PERSONALITY SURVIVES DEATH

After-Death Communication from Sir William Barrett

PERSONALITY SURVIVES DEATH

After-Death Communication
from Sir William Barrett

by
FLORENCE ELIZABETH BARRETT

www.whitecrowbooks.com

Personality Survives Death
Original Text, Copyright © 1937 by Florence Elizabeth Barrett.

This Copyright © 2020 by White Crow Productions Ltd. All rights reserved.
"Remembering Sir William Barrett," Copyright © 2020
by Michael Tymn. All rights reserved.

Published by White Crow Books; an imprint of White Crow Productions Ltd.

The right of Florence Elizabeth Barrett and Michael Tymn to be identified as the authors of this work has been asserted in accordance with the Copyright, Design and Patents act 1988.

No part of this book may be reproduced, copied or used in any form
or manner whatsoever without written permission, except in the
case of brief quotations in reviews and critical articles.

For information, contact White Crow Books by e-mail: info@whitecrowbooks.com.

Cover Design by Astrid@Astridpaints.com
Interior design by Velin@Perseus-Design.com

Paperback: ISBN: 978-1-78677-123-0
eBook ISBN: 978-1-78677-124-7

Non-Fiction / Body, Mind & Spirit / Spiritualism / Death & Dying

www.whitecrowbooks.com

Disclaimer: White Crow Productions Ltd. and its directors, employees, distributors, retailers, wholesalers and assignees disclaim any liability or responsibility for the author's statements, words, ideas, criticisms or observations.

Contents

Remembering Sir William Barrett vii
Foreword xiii
The Deeper Issues of Psychical Research xxiii
Introductory Note xxxix
Chapter 1 1
Chapter 2 7
Chapter 3 17
Chapter 4 27
Chapter 5 37
Chapter 6 41
Chapter 7 53
Chapter 8 65
Chapter 9 75
Chapter 10 83
Chapter 11 89
Chapter 12 97
Chapter 13 111
Chapter 14 121
Chapter 15 131
Chapter 16 137
Chapter 17 147
Chapter 18 153
Chapter 19 165
Epilogue 175

Remembering Sir William Barrett

Sir William Fletcher Barrett (February 10, 1844 – May 26, 1925) was one of the pioneers of psychical research. It was Barrett's idea to form the Society for Psychical Research (SPR) in London in 1882. However, since Barrett was living in Dublin, Ireland at the time, he was not able to take an active part in managing the Society. He left that up to three Cambridge scholars, Henry Sedgwick, Frederic W. H. Myers, and Edmund Gurney. Barrett also encouraged Professor William James of Harvard to organize the American branch of the SPR in 1884. He edited the SPR Journal from 1884-99 and served as president of the SPR in 1904.

Born in Jamaica, British West Indies, Barrett moved to England during his youth and studied under the famous physicist, John Tyndall, serving as Tyndall's assistant from 1862 to1867. He lectured on physics at the Royal School of Naval Architecture before becoming professor of physics at the Royal College of Science in Dublin in 1873. He taught at the Royal College for 37 years, retiring in 1910, and was knighted in 1912.

In 1899, Barrett developed a silicon-iron alloy known as stalloy, used in the commercial development of the telephone and transformers, and also did pioneering research on entoptic vision, leading to the invention of the entoptiscope and a new optometer. He was a fellow of the Royal Society, Philosophical Society, Royal Society of Literature as well as a member of the Institute of Electrical Engineers and the Royal Irish Academy.

Barrett began to take an interest in psychic phenomena in 1874 after hearing of the research of renowned scientist William Crookes (later Sir William) with mediums. "In fact I began the whole investigation of these phenomena convinced that [mal-observation or hallucination] was their true explanation, and it was not until after stretching this hypothesis to illegitimate lengths that I found the actual facts completely shattered my theory," Barrett explained his early views.[1]

Then 29, Barrett began experimenting with hypnosis, more popularly known as "mesmerism" in those days. He observed a young girl under hypnosis correctly identify a playing card randomly taken from a pack and placed in a book that was put next to her head. He also observed another hypnotized person correctly identify fourteen cards taken at random from a pack. As a scientist, he found such results very disturbing. However, while many of his scientific colleagues simply scoffed at anything paranormal, Barrett was open-minded and determined to find some rational and scientific explanation. As he explained his 1917 book *On the Threshold of the Unseen*, his prior theories really began to fall apart sometime in 1876 when a prominent English solicitor (lawyer) named Clark spent the summer at a residence near his in Dublin. Clark's 10-year-old daughter, Florrie, produced various paranormal phenomena, including levitations and spirit "raps" that spelled out messages from an "intelligence" calling himself "Walter."

As a result of his experiments in hypnosis and his investigation of Florrie Clark, Barrett prepared a paper to deliver to the British Association for the Advancement of Science. The Association rejected the paper as well as Barrett's request to present it orally to the group. After Crookes, Alfred Russel Wallace (co-originator with Charles Darwin of the natural selection theory of evolution),

---

[1] Barrett, Sir William, *On the Threshold of the Unseen*, E.P. Dutton & Co., 1918, p. 37

and Lord Rayleigh protested the Association's action, Barrett was allowed to deliver the paper but not publish it.

Barrett continued his investigation with other mediums, including Hester Travers Smith, Gladys Osborne Leonard, Kathleen Goligher, and Geraldine Cummins. In his 1917 book, he recalled the sitting with Goligher, who was being studied then by Dr. William Crawford of Queen's University. The sitting involved a small family circle gathered in a room illuminated with a bright gas flame burning in a lantern. "They sat round a small table with hands joined together, but no one touching the table," Barrett explained. "Very soon knocks came and messages were spelt out as one of us repeated the alphabet aloud. Suddenly the knocks increased in violence, and being encouraged, a tremendous bang came which shook the room and resembled the blow of a sledge hammer on an anvil. A tin trumpet which had been placed below the table now poked out its smaller end close under the top of the table near where I was sitting. I was allowed to try and catch it, but it dodged all my attempts in the most amusing way, the medium on the opposite side sat perfectly still, while at my request all held up their joined hands so that I could see no one was touching the trumpet, as it played peep-boo with me. Sounds like the sawing of wood, the bouncing of a ball, and other noises occurred, which were inexplicable."[2]

The table then began to rise from the floor some 18 inches and remained suspended in the air. "I was allowed to go up to the table and saw clearly no one was touching it, a clear space separating the sitters from the table," Barrett continued the explanation. "I tried to press the table down, and though I exerted all my strength could not do so; then I climbed up on the table and sat on it, my feet off the floor, when I was swayed to and fro and finally tipped off. The table of its own accord now turned upside down, no one touching it, and I tried to lift it off the ground, but it could not be stirred, it appeared screwed down to the floor. At my request all the sitters' clasped hands had been kept raised above their heads, and I could see that no one was touching the table. When I desisted from trying to lift the inverted table from the floor, it righted itself again on its own accord, no one helping it. Numerous sounds displaying an amused

---

[2] _____ p. 47

intelligence then came, and after each individual present had been greeted with some farewell raps the sitting ended."[3]

Barrett said that he could not imagine how the cleverest conjurer could have performed what he experienced, especially since it was clear to him that there was no elaborate apparatus in the room. Moreover, Dr. Crawford had been observing the Goligher circle for six months or more before his observations. "That there is an unseen intelligence behind these manifestations is all we can say, but that is a tremendous assertion, and if admitted destroys the whole basis of materialism," Barrett added.[4]

During his 50 years of studying psychic phenomena, Barrett observed nearly every type of mediumship. In his reminiscences, read at a private meeting of the SPR on June 17, 1924, less than a year before his death, Barrett said: "I am personally convinced that the evidence we have published decidedly demonstrates (*1*) the existence of a spiritual world, (2) survival after death, and (3) of occasional communication from those who have passed over… It is however hardly possible to convey to others who have not had a similar experience an adequate idea of the strength and cumulative force of the evidence that has compelled [my] belief."[5]

Barrett is also remembered for his study of dowsing and deathbed visions. His book, *Deathbed Visions*, first published in 1926, the year after his death, is still popular today. It offers a number of intriguing reports in which a dying person appears to see and recognize some deceased relative or friend, some of them involving instances where the dying person was unaware of the previous death of the spirit form he sees. "These cases form, perhaps, one of the most cogent arguments for survival after death, as the evidential value and veridical (truth telling) character of these visions of the dying is greatly enhanced when the fact is undeniably established that the dying person was wholly ignorant of the decease of the person he or she so vividly sees," Barrett stated in the Introduction.[6]

---

[3] _____ p. 48

[4] _____ p. 49

[5] Barrett, Sir William, *Deathbed Visions*, The Aquarian Press, 1986, p.162

[6] _____ p. 1

Several weeks after his death, Barrett's wife, Lady Florence Barrett, a prominent, obstetric surgeon and dean of the London School of Medicine for Women, began receiving very evidential messages from Sir William through the mediumship of Mrs. Leonard. Over the next eleven years, she sat with Leonard every few months, taking verbatim notes as Sir William communicated. She also received evidential messages from several other mediums. This book, *Personality Survives Death*, first published in 1937 by Longmans, Green and Co. of London, resulted from these sittings.

Lady Barrett asked Sir William how she might satisfy people that she was really talking to him. He replied that it depends on the type of mind, commenting that reference to a tear in the wallpaper in his old room might satisfy some people and not others. Lady Barrett noted that a month before his death he had pointed out a tear in the wallpaper in one corner of his room. Sir William then said that some higher minds have gone well beyond the need for such trivial verification, mentioning another distinguished British physicist, still in the flesh, Sir Oliver Lodge. "Lodge is nearer the bigger, greater aspect of things than most," he stated.[7]

Sir William further explained that his objective in communicating with his wife was not simply to add to the mass of evidence already given concerning the survival of consciousness at death but to help find a working philosophy to guide those on Earth who are struggling with finding a purpose in life. "It seems to me from where I am most people are not even struggling but meandering on purposelessly, blindly, because they have no definite philosophy as a starting point," he communicated.[8] He went on to say that knowledge of the afterlife opens the gates of inspiration and makes the intuition keener. With that comes greater enthusiasm, greater understanding of the beauties of life, even the perceiving of beauty where ugliness had appeared to exist.

---

[7] Barrett, Lady Florence, *Personality Survives Death*, Longmans, Green and Co., 1937, p. 14

[8] _____ p. 23

"Life on my side seems so extraordinarily easy compared to Earth," Sir William offered in a 1929 sitting, "because we simply live according to the rules of love."[9]

Michael Tymn,
January 2020

---

[9] _____ p. 104

Foreword

By Canon R. J. Campbell, D. D.

The contents of this small volume consist almost entirely of what purport to be communications from the late Sir William Barrett, F.R.S., to his wife through the mediumship of Mrs. Osborne Leonard. As such they are worthy of the serious attention of an intelligent and cultured public, partly because of their presumed source and partly because of their subject matter.

These scripts are not open to the reproach of triviality that is so often and so justly levelled against soi-disant spiritistic messages. They can stand the test of critical investigation on their own internal evidence, and the conditions under which they were produced were of the strictest scientific precision. The recorder, Lady Barrett, is not a person whom it would be easy to deceive in particular relating to a matter so vital as the identity of the communicator with the personality of her deceased husband, still less in the verisimilitude of the statements herein recorded when compared with Sir William's ways of expressing himself to those who knew him well during his earthly life. Her professional standing is sufficient witness to her competence in this respect. Hers is a keen scientifically trained intellect: she has attained the highest eminence in her profession and has held the most responsible positions in connection therewith for which women are eligible. I need say no more on this point.

Any reader who will take the trouble to acquaint himself with the salient facts of Lady Barrett's distinguished professional and public career will agree that an abler and more scrupulous note-taker and appraiser of the value of what is here given to the world would be hard to find. She has honoured me by asking me to write a foreword to what she has come to feel is material of sufficient importance to be regarded as of more than merely private interest. I comply with goodwill as it affords me the opportunity of paying a tribute of respect and affection to the memory of a man with whom I was privileged to be on terms of close personal intimacy for many years. From the standpoint of psychical research my credentials are less sure, but they are not entirely negligible. I have been an associate of the Society for Psychical Research for about thirty-five years, though in all that time I have only attended one meeting of the Society. I subscribed to it in order to obtain and study the Proceedings month by month, and I think I can claim without presumption to have done this pretty thoroughly. But it is chiefly owing to Sir William Barrett himself that I have retained my interest in the subject and have come to share his conclusion that difficult, baffling and elusive though the phenomena with which it deals undoubtedly are, they do furnish positive proof that man is more than can be accounted for in terms of his physical organisation. I believe also, again with Sir William, that communication does occasionally take place between the living and the so-called dead. Psychical research is thus capable of rendering good service to religion, though it is no substitute for it, as no one has more firmly and consistently pointed out than Sir William Barrett himself again and again. During his whole mature life he was a devout and earnest Christian and he died a communicant of the Church of England. Of his eminence as a man of science there is no need to write, but neither should it be overlooked in issuing a book of this kind, which may fall into the hands of some who are ignorant of his important contributions to scientific knowledge and their practical application to industry. As Professor of Physics in the Royal College of Science at Dublin for nearly forty years he became known for his investigations on sensitive flames, and was the discoverer of the alloy to which he gave the name of 'stalloy,' and which has been of great and ever-growing service to electrical engineering. His researches and experiments in iron alloys continued for many years with enormous benefit to metallic invention and enterprise, notably in the application of the nickel-iron compound, now entitled 'permalloy,' to the casing of long-distance submarine cables. In another field, that of entoptic vision, his patient and successful pioneer work led to the invention of the entoptiscope and a new type of optometer. Not so well known as it ought to be is the fact that what Sir William added to scientific knowledge of the magnetic and electrical properties of certain alloys has had a considerable bearing upon the development of telephony in all its branches. This is only the briefest possible summary of his achievements in his own department of science, but is sufficient to show that his qualifications as an investigator of any kind of phenomena were of a high order.

His interest in psychical research dates very far back. I have heard him state that it arose in the first instance out of his experience as a physicist. He found the psychical factor constantly impinging upon his familiar acquaintance with the operation of the laws governing material facts. As long ago as 1872 or 1873 he had become convinced that the psychical factor in evolution could not be ignored and would have to be reckoned with in any thorough effort to understand the development of life and mind upon this planet. It was in 1874 that he took up the subject seriously and systematically, stimulated thereto by the revelations of Professor (later Sir William) Crookes concerning his experiments with Florence Cook. Some first-hand experiences of supernormal phenomena on the part of Barrett himself lent additional force to what he had heard from Crookes, and caused him to revise his earlier theory that Crookes might have been mildly hypnotised when making his extraordinary observations. This change of attitude was followed by Barrett taking the bold course of reading a paper before the British Association in Glasgow in 1876, detailing his personal experiences of some bizarre phenomena similar to, though not so starkly challenging as, those recorded by Crookes. As is now well known, this paper was no more favourably received than that of Crookes had been, and the Association refused to print it. The purpose of the paper was to obtain support if possible for the appointment of a scientific committee to inquire into and report upon the validity or otherwise of what are now usually called psychical phenomena. It failed at the moment, but in 1881 Barrett took the initiative in bringing into existence the Society for Psychical Research, whose first president was the eminent Professor Sidgwick, and whose most active members for a long period were F. W. H. Myers and Edmund Gurney. The Society was actually constituted in January 1882. At a much later date Barrett became the principal mover in the establishment of similar societies in Canada and the United States of America.

From the beginning the British society was fortunate in the number of exceptionally distinguished men who took part in its deliberations. Among these were Mr. A. J. Balfour (afterwards Earl Balfour) and his brother, the present Earl. Mr. Gladstone was an honorary member and expressed himself in an oft-quoted dictum as satisfied that the work the Society was attempting was of transcendent importance. On the death of the great statesman in 1899 the Council of the S.P.R. elected Barrett an honorary member in succession to him, a compliment that Barrett always felt to be one of the most gratifying he ever received. Myers' letter conveying the intimation reads as follows:

> My dear Barrett, Bennett will have informed you officially that the Council of the S.P.R. unanimously elected you a successor to Gladstone as Honorary Member; but I want to add my personal expression of pleasure at having been able to take part in the well-earned compliment. May your name long stand on our front page! The front page of the Society which you more than anyone founded.
> Yours ever,
> F. W. H. Myers.

Among the distinguished men of science who gave their countenance to the new venture, none was more warmly esteemed than Professor G. J. Romanes. In an autograph letter, dated December 8, 1882, Romanes says to Barrett:

> *If the alleged phenomena are true* [phrase underlined by Romanes], I hold it to be unquestionable that they would be of more importance than any other to the science and philosophy of our time; and therefore, by parity of reasoning, in whatever measure they are taken to be possibly true, in that measure does an inquiry into their truth become important.

In an earlier letter (October 28) Romanes states:

> I should very much like to join your Society, if by doing so I could get access to any of your committees of inquiry. I should work well and without prejudice for I have become very much staggered about the whole subject, and so feel that for me it has assumed more importance than any other.

There had been previous attempts of a similar kind which achieved little of permanent value. The Psychological Society, founded in 1875, of which Serjeant Cox was a leading spirit, owed its inception to the interest awakened in a limited circle by the supranormal experiments of Professor Crookes in what became known as the 'Katie King' series, his own laboratory being the séance room and the young woman, Florence Cook, the medium for the production of the phenomena under examination. This society ceased to exist in 1879, perhaps because its purview had been insufficiently well defined. A quarter of a century earlier a similar sporadic effort had been made on the initiative of the Rev. B. F. Westcott, afterwards Bishop of Durham.

The 'Ghost Society,' as it was called, did not attract much support from scientific men. Very likely it was premature, and the name given to it would deter some serious minds from co-operation with its object, which appears in the main to have been the collection of reliable facts pertaining to the mysterious borderland which has always been known to exist between everyday human life and the beyond. The facts with which the Society sought to deal were substantially the same as those which the Society for Psychical Research was afterwards founded to inquire into, but the approach to them was not as carefully mapped. Barrett and his group of friends insisted from the first that before any useful conclusion could be arrived at relating to the possible survival of personality after death it would be necessary to clear the ground by exploring what was possible in the way of communication between one incarnate mind and another apart from the usual channels of sense. Contrary to popular assumption the Society for Psychical Research was not founded merely to sift the evidence for or against the validity of the claims of Spiritualism, but to examine into and endeavour to obtain scientific knowledge of the obscure processes and potentialities of human personality, a wide field that up to 1882 had been comparatively neglected, though it is now the special territory of psychologists of various schools. The stimulus communicated by the S.P.R. to students of paranormal human faculty has been strong and productive. Psychology and psychotherapy owe much to its painstaking pioneer work. Barrett's special contribution to the data of the Society, and in a measure to its definite findings, if one may single out a department of the Society's inquiries wherein he eventually became the chief authority, was his succession of reports on Dowsing. There is no need to summarise these, they are easily accessible in the records of the S.P.R. It suffices to say that what was formerly regarded as no more than a fantastic or at the best illusory gift to be classed with that of the gypsy fortune-teller is now recognised as a genuine if still unexplained cryptic endowment of certain individuals.

Barrett never made the mistake of over-emphasising the worth of the vast amount of evidence he and his colleagues were instrumental in accumulating as pointing in the direction of demonstrating the persistence of self-consciousness, memory and individuality after physical death. As long ago as October 29, 1881, he wrote in *Light*:

> I cordially recognise the fact that in bereavement and deep distress numbers have been cheered and consoled by the hope that Spiritualism has set before them. Nevertheless loyalty to truth compels me to acknowledge the evil and the good that have come under my own observation; the evil when Spiritualism is made a stepping stone down to

a lower plane, the good when it is used as a stepping stone to something higher. But it will be said; can we not find a religion, and so rest, in the teaching of Spiritualism? My own strong conviction is that we cannot; that is, if we are true to the highest instincts of our nature, to those divine intuitions and admonitions which come to every soul struggling into light. And this conviction is not the result of any preconceived opinion, but of wide observation conducted with an honest desire to know the truth.

'By their fruits ye shall know them.' Weighed in the balances, Spiritualism *as a religion* [italics his] is found wanting, for it is unable to satisfy the highest needs of man.

From this conviction he never swerved, as I for one can testify from repeated conversations with him on the subject. In his preface to a book by the Rev. Donald Hole, entitled *Love and Death*, published in 1922, he said:

Neither in Pagan nor in Christian literature do we find that Spiritualism (or its equivalent) had added to the intellectual or moral advancement of the race. On the other hand we find a singular consensus of opinion amongst Christians, in all times, of distrust and aversion to the whole subject. There must be some reason for this hostility, or prejudice as some would call it.

After mentioning some of the reasons, such as the amount of trickery connected with the subject, and the danger of moral deterioration not infrequently observed in those who become absorbed in it, he goes on to state:

This being the case, Spiritualism becomes a treacherous quicksand upon which to build a new religion.

It is also significant that we seldom, if ever, receive any veridical (truth telling) messages from the many saintly souls who have passed to the unseen; it may be that the tendrils of attachment to the present life need to be severed before the soul can rise to a higher life, or gain the beatific vision.

His own fine Christian character is the best commentary on the wisdom and rightness of these and other pronouncements of the same tenour. He did not depend upon psychical research for what he felt to be most precious in life. His faith in God, his devotion to our Lord Jesus Christ, his life of prayer and service would have been what they were if psychical research had never been heard of. He was one of the most lovable of men, and his simple sunny goodness of heart won him a host of friends. His sociability was one of his most marked characteristics; he liked mingling with people of all ranks and classes, and no trouble or sacrifice were too great if thereby he could do a kindness or assist a worthy cause. Numbers of persons who have done well in life are glad to owe their start to his unselfish zeal on their behalf, and almost every effort for the social benefit of the unprivileged in our time received his warm and enthusiastic support.

It has been remarked that he had a childlike and guileless nature which evoked the best in others and habitually expected it. This was quite true, but it is no less true that this quality consisted with what amounted at times to astonishing insight into the motives of those with whom he came in contact. I have not seen attention drawn to this anywhere, but no one who knew him well could fail to be impressed by it. He never made an uncharitable observation, but a word of warning quietly dropped from his lips has on occasion saved a friend from trusting too readily to appearances in regard to the dependability of a casual acquaintance. His intuitive judgments were always right.

He married late in life, but no union of souls could have been more perfect than was that he enjoyed to the end with the wife who survives him and through whom what she believes to be these messages from him are now given to the world. This small selection from a very much larger amount of material has been made with care and discrimination. Doubtless if matters of purely private and

FOREWORD

personal interest had not been excluded, more of what a journalist would call the human appeal would have been felt by the reader.

But this is not Lady Barrett's object, nor would it consort with either her or her late husband's wish. Except for the omission of matters, sometimes of a particularly striking and evidential character, but of a bearing too intimate and domestic to be accorded a place in these pages, the actual editorship exercised has been of the slightest. The scripts consist for the most part, though not entirely, of the trance utterances of Mrs. Osborne Leonard. On the rare occasions where the medium is another person the fact is stated in the text. The supposed 'control' who speaks through Mrs. Leonard's lips is said to be an ancestress of hers whom she calls by the name of Feda. Feda may be a secondary personality of Mrs. Leonard herself, but to admit this does not invalidate the claim of the messages to emanate from a discarnate source. Feda speaks for Sir William, not infrequently employing the first person as though Sir William in person were dictating the words. Occasionally, but very rarely, a word or sentence is interjected in what purports to be his own direct voice apart altogether from the medium. This is a startling phenomenon, but well attested. Where such a word or sentence occurs it is noted in the report of the sitting. The bulk of the communications, however, are as aforesaid given through the medium's control and taken down verbatim by Lady Barrett.

The only modification she has made in her transcript of these records is in ignoring some of the control's peculiarities of diction. To have reproduced these would have added nothing to the sense of what is conveyed, and would have had the disadvantage of detracting from the smooth readableness of the statements made in Sir William Barrett's name. It should be added that these are far above the normal capacity of Mrs. Osborne Leonard's mind and interests in life, though members of the S.P.R., on the other hand, have been for many years fully satisfied of her unimpeachable *bona fides*. The contents of the scripts speak for themselves.

Reprinted from the Contemporary Review, February, 1918.

The Deeper Issues of Psychical Research[10]

'Is anything of God's contriving endangered by enquiry? Was it the system of the universe or the monks that trembled at the telescope of Galileo? Did the circulation of the firmament stop in terror because Newton laid his daring finger on its pulse?'

~ Lowell.

It is significant of the change of thought which has taken place in recent years that your Society has asked me to address you on the subject of Psychical Research, an honour for which I am both surprised and grateful, and the more so at the inclusion

---

[10] The substance of an address delivered by Sir William Barrett, F.R.S., to the Clerical Society of the Diocese of Birmingham, Bishop Hamilton Baynes presiding.

of a humble layman like myself in your lecture list of eminent ecclesiastics.

The term psychical research is much misunderstood. It is often considered to be only another name for ghost hunting, spooks, and necromancy, and either dismissed with a shrug and a sneer or condemned as unlawful. Let me therefore say at the outset that the objects of this research were defined in the original statement of the Society, which first used the term, and has now published some forty-five volumes of its proceedings and journal since its foundation in 1882.

These objects were the critical examination of:

(1) The alleged action of mind upon mind, independently of the recognised channels of sense; thought-transference, now included in the wider term telepathy.
(2) The phenomena of hypnotism.
(3) The transcendental perceptive power, or clairvoyance, asserted to exist in certain sensitives.
(4) First-hand evidence for veridical (truth-telling) apparitions of the living or dying.
(5) The alleged physical phenomena of Spiritualism; and (6) Historical evidence bearing on these subjects.

'The aim of the Society,' it is stated, 'will be to approach these various questions without prejudice, and in the same spirit of exact and unimpassioned enquiry which has enabled science to solve so many problems, once not less obscure nor less hotly debated.' It will be observed that nothing is stated about obtaining experimental evidence for survival after death, a question only attacked by the Society in subsequent years; albeit as the Right Hon. A. J. Balfour remarked in his Presidential address to the Society in 1894: 'All arbitrary limitations of our sphere of work are to be avoided. ... If beyond the mere desire to increase knowledge many are animated by the wish to get evidence, not through any process of laborious deduction, but by direct observation of the reality of intelligences not endowed with a physical organisation like our own, I see nothing in their action to criticise, much less to condemn.'

There are of course some educated persons who doubt the validity of the conclusions many of us have reached, because the numerous psychical phenomena upon which those conclusions are based cannot be reproduced with certainty at any given time or place.

Neither can we reproduce at will fireballs, or other meteoric phenomena, nor many pathological conditions; for these, and other sporadic phenomena, we are content to accept the testimony of accredited observers. 'Nothing can destroy the evidence of testimony in any case,' Bishop Butler points out, 'but a proof or probability that persons are not competent judges of the facts to which they gave testimony.' Records of observations and experiments depend for their acceptance on the probity and intelligence of the persons recording them, and 'it is impossible for us,' as Professor Henry Sidgwick once remarked, 'or any other investigators, to demonstrate to persons who do not know us that we are not idiotically careless or consciously mendacious.' It is hardly necessary to dwell on the difference between demonstrating physical and psychical phenomena. The former are not affected by the will or other psychical conditions, the latter depend on those conditions. Certain persons, not characterised by hysteria or neurotic symptoms, or by any class, age or sex distinction, are found to be sensitive to psychical impressions to which others are insensitive. They constitute the intermediaries or subjects, through whose organisation phenomena otherwise unperceived by us become perceptible. There is nothing improbable in this; we find an analogy in the limited range of our senses and how that range varies in different individuals.

There are waves in the air and in the ether too long or too short for our senses to detect. These waves can be revealed and examined by appropriate physical intermediaries, such as a photographic plate or the receiver in wireless telegraphy, etc. We do not disbelieve in the use of a fluorescent screen to reveal the X-rays, although it may be called a 'medium' whereby the unseen is translated into the seen.

We know very little as yet of the physiological or psychological causes that enable some persons to be a reagent, or medium, to psychical impressions which do not affect others. This much seems probable, that the former belong to a class called by Professor Pierre Janet *les individus suggestibles*. That is to say, they respond readily to any impression or suggestion coming from within or without their organism; the idea or suggestion may arise from their own subconsciousness, or from their environment, or from the mind of a living person, or from a discarnate mind – assuming such to exist.

Something typical of this suggestibility of certain individuals and not of others is seen in many of the lower forms of life. It is well known that certain lizards, fishes, and shrimps, even certain caterpillars and chrysalises, will change their natural colour to suit their environment. The majority of creatures in the same natural order are not thus affected. In the susceptible, or suggestible, individuals the stimulus of a coloured light sets up a reflex action in their nervous system, which, in some unknown way, automatically modifies the colour of the pigment secreted by the caterpillar or chrysalis, enabling a protective coloration to be assumed. How far this special sensitiveness of particular individuals, or varieties, in the lower forms of life extends to cognitive impressions we do not know.

Many insects, as the naturalist Fabre has shown, have some unknown means of cognition, which transcends all recognised channels of sense.

Recognising the fact that a good psychical subject or medium is more or less influenced by his environment, it is obvious that psychical phenomena may be inhibited by the presence of flippant or hostile investigators. Interested and sympathetic attention, without credulity, is desirable on the part of the enquirer. Do we not find the same condition governing our access to the higher spiritual world? Every religious teacher knows that a lack of interest or reverence, still more an atmosphere of doubt and suspicion in his listeners, will render the most earnest spiritual appeal barren and ineffective. Speaking only of the psychical order, Mr. C. G. Massey said 'Faith is the key to the gate of the invisible world.' Upon this a well-known Spiritualist, the Rev. Stainton Moses (M.A. Oxon.), remarked: 'What Mr. Massey calls "faith" is a predisposition and attention, a sympathetic state of mind, which establishes between an observer and a medium a *rapport*, without which no results are to be had that are worth having.[11] It is easy to scoff at this, for everyone knows that success in business, science or warfare, does not depend upon any *rapport* between ourselves and the material world. But those who have had any true spiritual experience, know the meaning of this *rapport* in communion with the unseen, and that faith is really the key to the gate of the invisible world, which prayer unlocks.

Much of the difficulty which is felt by the educated world in accepting the evidence of supernormal phenomena – supernatural is a misnomer – arises from the fact that we habitually think of our senses as the only possible channels of awakening perception. We associate all our feelings and consciousness with our sensory organs and our material brain. In spite of philosophy and religion many find it difficult to believe that when the brain perishes the mind and our perceptive power will not also perish. But consciousness, instead of being limited to the brain, is more probably limited by the brain; which may be only, as Professor William James has suggested, an apparatus for the transmission of a wider consciousness external to ourselves. The brain is not the source of consciousness, but only a terrestrial means of its manifestation. The glowing filament of an electric lamp is not the source of the electric energy, it is only the means by which that energy is transmitted and rendered manifest. Nor is the field of electric force confined to the transmitting wire, it extends through the ether of space around the wire. In like manner our mind can exist and extend its action beyond the material brain. There remains, however, the mystery of self-consciousness, of human personality, which is something more fundamental and individual than a universal consciousness variously tinted by transmission through human brains. That mystery it is unlikely we can ever solve.

The opposition to psychical research shown by those who are imbued with the German materialistic habit of thought is very natural. Vociferous Sadducees like Mr. Edward Clodd, or ferocious, though amusing, sceptics like Dr. Mercier, realise that the admission even of telepathy would place them on the slope that leads to the abyss

---

[11] Here one is reminded of our Lord's words on the inhibitory effect of unbelief on His miraculous powers (Matt, xiii, 58; and xvii, 20).

where their cherished opinions would be engulfed. 'Of the reality of telepathy,' one of our most eminent psychologists, Dr. W. McDougall, F.R.S., says in his masterly work *Body and Mind* (p. 349), 'it is of such a nature as to compel the assent of any competent person who studies it impartially.' But this is exactly what our opponents will not do, neither will they take the trouble to conduct an experimental investigation of a subject which requires long and laborious care. Instructive criticism is always welcome, but mere denial on a priori grounds alone is of no more value than a yokel denying that iron exists in the sun.

The discovery of wireless telegraphy has doubtless rendered telepathy less improbable to many. But a similar quasi-mechanical transmission of 'brain waves,' as some have suggested, is inadmissible, though it might conciliate opponents and be compatible with a mechanistic view of the mind. This is worth a moment's consideration.

All radiant forces, such as light, heat, gravitation, etc., when freely diffused through space diminish in intensity as the square of the distance increases between the source and the receiver, if no absorbing medium intervenes. At a thousand feet apart the intensity is a million times less than at one foot apart. To transmit a wireless message across the Atlantic therefore requires a very powerful source of electric waves and a very sensitive receiver. Now there are well attested cases of telepathy occurring between individuals, not only thousands of feet apart, but thousands of miles asunder – if apparitions at or near the time of death are due to a telepathic impression, as seems probable – a phantasm being projected from the mind of the percipient. Yet, in such cases, there was no exhaustion, no exertion even, on the part of the unconscious source of these imaginary brain waves.

It is therefore highly improbable that telepathy is transmitted by waves radiating in every direction, like light from a candle. Nor can we conceive of unwritten or unspoken thought being carried by a messenger, or sent through a conduit, or fired like a bullet at a target.

Moreover, in telepathy ideas and feelings, more frequently than exact words, impress the percipient.

There is abundant evidence that emotions and sensations such as pain, taste, etc., experienced by one person are simultaneously felt by a distant percipient, under conditions that exclude the possibility of fraud or any verbal communication. The remarkable fact is also coming to light, that telepathy is not ultimately due to any conscious and voluntary operation of the mind, either in the originating or receiving personality, such as occurs in the ordinary operation of speech or writing.

Telepathy, then, cannot be explained by a process of mechanical transmission. It appears to be a case of 'action at a distance.' But physicists do not admit action at a distance as an ultimate fact, although the attracting influence of one body upon another throughout the realms of space appears to be such an action.

Gravitation, however, is not likely to be an exception to other physical forces, though we may have to wait a long time for its satisfactory explanation. Telepathy and gravitation are only alike in this; that at present we are ignorant how two different masses, and how two different minds, at a distance apart, can transmit their influence. The two operations are in wholly different categories – one belongs to the physical order, the other to the psychical order.

It may be, as my friend Mr. F. C. Constable suggested in his work *Personality and Telepathy*, that we may find in telepathy evidence of the direct operation of a transcendental part of our being which is not conditioned in matter, time, or space. In any case, telepathy and its implications will afford a profound and fruitful subject of psychological discussion in the near future. Mrs. Henry Sidgwick has pointed out that:

> Telepathy, if a purely psychical process – and the reasons for thinking it is so increase – indicates that the mind can work independently of the body, and thus adds to the probability that it can survive it. Increased knowledge about the subliminal self, by giving glimpses of extension of human faculty and showing that there is more of us than we are nominally aware of, similarly suggests that the limitations imposed by our bodies and our material surroundings are temporary limitations.[12]

---

[12] Proceedings of the S.P.R., vol. xxix, p. 247.

I will return to the evidence psychical research has afforded of the first part of this quotation presently, but before doing so it is necessary to explain what is meant by what Frederic Myers termed the subliminal self. Below the *limen*, or threshold, of consciousness there are within us all faculties and activities which far transcend our knowledge or conscious power.

Our personality has been well compared to the solar radiation, of which only a fraction is visible in the rainbow-tinted spectrum of sunlight. Beyond the red, at one side, and beyond the blue, at the other side, there are multitudes of invisible rays, which can be rendered perceptible by appropriate means. Each pencil of the sun's rays carries with it a trinity of benediction to this Earth. The visible rays illuminate the world and reveal the glory of nature, the longer invisible waves warm the Earth and give us all our wind and water-power, the shorter invisible waves, beyond the blue, cover the Earth with vegetation, and thus feed man and beast. What is visible is not only the smallest part of the flux of energy streaming from the sun, but it is the least permanent. The invisible part of the solar radiation, which bathed the Earth in ages long past, lives with us today – on the one hand, it warms and illuminates our rooms, and, on the other, it has helped to mould the surface of the Earth; compared with these invisible rays, which science has revealed, the visible sunlight of the past was only a beautiful and transitory episode. So, too, in our human personality the smaller, and perhaps the least permanent part, is that self of which we are now conscious.

Our bodily, subconscious life is, of course, recognised by all; it controls the circulation and respiration, the nutrition and reparation of our body. None of these functions could we perform by voluntary action, even with the utmost knowledge and will of our conscious self. These amazing subconscious activities have doubt less been acquired by slow degrees in the course of evolution. But what directs and coordinates the function of the myriad cell-life within the living body? Physico-chemical processes are, of course, in operation, reflex nervous action is always taking place, but how can we explain, except by some intelligent selection, such established facts as the renewal of the severed limbs of a newt, or the regeneration of the lens of its eye from the iris, when the lens has been removed? May there not be, as Mr. Gerald Balfour has suggested, a telepathic *rapport* between every living cell and the dominant centre of subconscious psychical activity; a *rapport* within the organism only impaired by disease and severed by death? Each cell would thus be like an obedient servant in a cooperative community, carrying out its appropriate task under some higher and intelligent direction. So we may conceive the human race as constituent cells, the many members, of one Body, to which all are related, and yet all transcended in one Immanent and Supreme Being. And may there not be some telepathic inter-communion between the Creator and all responsive human hearts, to some being given the inner ear, the open vision, and the inspired utterance? The subliminal *mental* life has, however, capacities which not only outstrip our conscious intelligence, but appear to transcend the limitations of our senses and of our organism. It is difficult otherwise to explain the supernormal perceptive power, or clairvoyance, indubitably possessed by certain persons, of which the lucidity of sensitives in deep hypnosis, and that of the 'dowser' (or subterranean water and ore finder) in the normal state, afford illustrations. Official science, it is true, does not admit the existence of this or any other supernormal faculty, nor acknowledge a subliminal self or its transcendental powers; but a growing and influential number of psychologists are returning to a belief in the existence of a soul in man. The soul is no longer 'out of fashion' in many high quarters of the scientific world.

Now there is undeniable evidence that sometimes, shortly before or after death, the human spirit can escape from the barrier of the brain and make its presence known to friends at a distance. Rarely is the conscious self aware of this excursive action of the soul, nor is it due to any conscious volition, except in so far as the desire may stimulate the subliminal activities. The cautiously worded conclusion arrived at by Professor and Mrs. Henry Sidgwick, after their critical and prolonged examination of this subject, states as a 'proved fact' that chance coincidence cannot account for the connection between deaths and veridical apparitions of the dying.

Nor is this freedom of the mind from the body confined to the time of death; as already mentioned, this fact is indicated if telepathy be a purely psychical process. Several persons, some of them well known to me, have desired to appear to a friend at a remote distance, who was unaware the experiment was about to be made, and have so appeared. The carefully conducted experiments which establish this fact have never been impugned so far as I know. If we admit telepathy, this fact is not much more wonderful than ordinary vision; for all the objects we see are only appearances or phantasms projected into space by our mind, and due to a certain tract of brain cells being stimulated by a series of minute impressions transmitted by the optic nerve from the retina.

There are, moreover, cases where telepathy merges into what Frederic Myers termed telergy, which differs from telepathy, as it is not merely an unknown mode of communication from one mind to another, but implies 'the direct influence of an extraneous spirit on the brain or organism of the percipient.' This may indeed be the case in many cases of telepathy between the living, the extraneous spirit being the soul or subliminal self of a distant living person. It is less familiar, but hardly less extraordinary, than the mysterious psycho-physical interaction which takes place daily between our own mind and body; telergy assumes that this habitual action is temporarily superseded by, or mingled with, the influence exerted by an extraneous mind. Hence in telergy the invading spirit or mind, acting through the brain of its new host, usurps for a time the control of the muscles of the percipient. What is called trance-speaking and automatic writing, or messages automatically spelt out by table-tilting, or by means of the so-called 'ouija board,' are either due to the normal subconscious action of the brain and mind of the medium, or supernormal cases wherein telepathy sometimes merges into telergy.

The following remarkable case illustrates what I have been saying; it resembles similar spiritualistic phenomena, but here the psychical invasion, or telergy, was from a living person who was asleep at the time and 130 miles distant. Although the circumstance took place some years ago, the evidential value of the case is very great, for the letters which narrate the facts were written at the time and are in my possession, with the envelopes and postmarks attesting the dates. I am permitted to give the names of the writers, to whom my thanks are due, and also to my niece, Mrs. Cowdell Barrett, of Weymouth, who put me in communication with her friends Mr. and Mrs. Arundel Mackenzie-Ashton, of Dene Court, Taunton.

The facts are, briefly, as follows: Mr. Mackenzie-Ashton, when a young man, went to stay at a vicarage in Nottinghamshire in September, 1882. After his visit he went to his parents' home in Hertfordshire, 130 miles away. Soon after he left the vicarage, Mr. (now Colonel) Nicholson and Mrs. Nicholson, with both of whom he was unacquainted, went to stay at the vicarage, and a few days later Mr. Mackenzie-Ashton received from Mr. Nicholson the following letter, which explains itself:

> September 14th, 1882.
> I have been staying at W— Vicarage lately, and last evening (Wednesday) we amused ourselves with 'table turning.' The table, when asked by whose spirit it was possessed, answered, 'Arundel Mackenzie'; and to the further question, 'Where is he?' it replied, 'His soul is here.' To the question, 'How is his body occupied?' it returned a perfectly definite answer. Would you mind informing me how you were occupied last night from 10.30 to 11.30 p.m., and in whose company you were, and what you were doing out of doors in the daytime? Pray excuse a perfect stranger asking you these impertinent questions, but I am anxious to be satisfied whether these 'manifestations' were true or false.

Mr. Mackenzie-Ashton, who had recently added the name 'Ashton' to Arundel Mackenzie, replied, giving the particulars asked for, and Mr. Nicholson then writes: 'Will you assure me on your word of honour that you had heard nothing whatever from any person at the Vicarage that evening?' This assurance was given, and then follows this letter from Mr. Nicholson: When I asked for your assurance I felt it was scarcely necessary, but the experience was so extraordinary that it seemed more satisfactory to have it.

We [naming the persons present at the Vicarage] had our hands on the table, which began immediately to move; on being asked to tilt if a spirit was present, it did so.

Asked, 'Whose spirit?' it replied [tilting at the right letter when the alphabet was repeated] and gave the answers named in the previous letter; asked, 'What is his body doing?' at first no reply was given. After waiting, we asked the same question again, and the reply was given, 'Playing billiards'; the time was then 11:15. p.m. asked 'Who is with him?' the answer was 'Father'; asked 'Who is winning?' answer 'Son.' Asked 'How many games have been played?' answer 'Two.' Asked 'What has he [A. Mackenzie] been doing during the day?' answer 'Shooting.' At this there was a general exclamation, 'Impossible!' for it was not believed that you had done any shooting, and H. asked, 'Pheasants or partridges?' laughing – but we could get no more. H., by request, left the table, and we asked the [soi-disant] spirit why it had not replied; it answered 'Flippant' and we could get no more. This is a literal and exact statement of what took place. A peculiar tremor ran through the table till the right letter was reached, and then the tilting was decided and distinct. The lights in the room were not lowered; the experience has thoroughly astonished me.

Highly improbable as it seemed to the sitters at the table, all the above particulars were perfectly correct.

Mr. A. Mackenzie-Ashton writes:

> I had been shooting during the day (Wednesday), and in the evening I had two games of billiards with my father. I won both of them, and after that I lay down on a couch in the billiard-room and fell asleep. Then I had a dream that I was back in W— Vicarage.

Of the trustworthiness of my informants and the accuracy of the narrative there can be no doubt, nor can the facts be explained away by chance coincidence, or by surreptitious knowledge on the part of the sitters at the Vicarage, who did not know that Mr. Mackenzie-Ashton was at the time visiting his parents 130 miles away. Here, then, we have evidence of what appears to be either telepathy from the subliminal personality of a sleeping person, or, more probably, telergy – the direct influence of an extraneous mind on the brain and organism of the distant sitters.

Nor is this case unique; somewhat similar instances are known to students of psychical research, and one has recently occurred in London, where the 'sitters' were personal friends of mine. These well attested facts of the mind acting independently of the body add to the probability that the mind survives the dissolution of the body, and that it can likewise (for a time, at any rate) give proof of its survival. From the confused memories of their earthly life, which constitute the bulk of communications that purport to come from the discarnate, it may be that some of these messages also proceed from a sleeping or semi-conscious dreaming state of the deceased person. If this be so, it would explain the common objection to the trivial and scrappy communications from the unseen, and that they are so often only fragmentary reminiscences of life on Earth.

On the other hand, it is by recalling definite facts known to us and to them that the identity of any person can be established. If a long absent friend speaks to us from a remote distance through the telephone we may recognise him by his voice, but if a stranger communicates for him, he will be asked to state more or less trivial incidents in the past life of our friend, which it is hoped we may recall in order to establish his identity. Our hesitation in accepting such statements appears to exasperate a discarnate, as it would any other communicator. As regards the former, our perplexity is increased by the frequent intrusion of ideas and memories from the subconsciousness of the medium, through whom the messages are delivered.

Nevertheless, sufficient proof of identity is sometimes given which cannot be attributed to any filching of ideas, or telepathic impressions, from those present.

Some instances of what seem to be unequivocal proof of identity are given in my recent book, *On the Threshold of the Unseen*.

Space will only allow me to refer to one such case. Here a message came through two esteemed personal friends of mine in Dublin, which purported to be from a cousin of one of my friends, an officer who had lost his life in the war. To prove his identity he asked that his personal effects, including a pearl tie-pin that he mentioned, should be given to a lady in London, whom he stated he was going to marry, giving her full Christian name and surname, which was an uncommon one. Neither of the sitters, nor any of the officer's own family in Ireland or elsewhere, knew he was going to marry, they had never heard this lady's name, nor that the officer possessed a pearl tie-pin. Later on, when the War Office sent over the deceased officer's effects, it was discovered that he had put down the lady's name in the will he had scribbled, as his next-of-kin; he gave her address in London, and both Christian and surname were precisely the same as those given in the message which had come through my friends four months previously; moreover, a pearl tie-pin was found among his effects. As the message was written down at the time it was given through my friends, and a copy sent to me, it seems impossible to find any other solution than a telepathic communication from the officer after his decease. But I admit that, however cogent the evidence, its interpretation is a matter of individual opinion.

There remains the strong objection, felt by both the Christian and the Jewish Church, to any attempt to lift even a corner of the veil that hides the unseen world from us. This repugnance rests, of course, upon the Biblical prohibition of necromancy. I have dealt fully with this question elsewhere, and can only make a passing reference to it here. These Biblical injunctions would doubtless apply to the whole range of psychical research, and were very wise and necessary before science had established a knowledge of the fact that, amidst the mutability and mystery of all things, there was no capriciousness, no disorder. Psychical enquiry in early ages would 'have lost itself in dark and difficult regions,' and produced a state of intellectual and moral confusion. Weariness and perplexity would have resulted, faith in the orderly government of the world would have been shaken, and the dictates of reason might have been supplanted by giving heed to an oracle. Isaiah saw this, and told the Jewish nation: Thy spells and enchantments, with which thou hast wearied thyself, have led thee astray.

To the ignorant and foolish these warnings are applicable today; and unbalanced minds need to be warned off a region which may prove such a treacherous quicksand. But contempt and condemnation of the whole subject are as mischievous as credulity and lack of common sense.

The psychical order, it is true, is not the spiritual order, but I am convinced that, as our knowledge of the former increases, it will confirm and throw light on the conditions of access to the spiritual world. Faith, as already stated, is the key to the gate of the invisible world, and if we wish to gain an entrance either to the outer or inner courts of that world, it is pre-requisite to have humility of spirit no less than confidence of hope. 'We lie,' as Emerson says, 'in the lap of immense Intelligence, which makes us receivers of its truth and organs of its activity. ... We can do nothing of ourselves but allow a passage to its beams.' Hence when 'two or three meet together' in calm and quiet expectation, sooner or later their involuntary perception and action will be quickened. But it is necessary to 'try the spirits,' or the mind of the percipient may be laid open to psychical invasion of a lower order. The cases of 'possession' narrated in the gospels, and known in all parts of the ancient and modern world, cannot, in every case, be explained away by hysteria or epilepsy, but are often, I believe, genuine instances of telergy, the influence of an extraneous spirit, whether incarnate or discarnate, on the organism of the sufferer.

There is also evidence in different branches of psychical research of a curious transmission of psychic power, or effluence (such as the older mesmerists asserted to exist), from its possessor to a hitherto passive and inert person. I have given instances of this in my monograph on the so-called 'dowsing-rod,' wherein a good dowser by touching an inert person transmits to him the singular 'gift' the dowser possesses. The same thing is often noticed in other cases of 'motor-automatism' and in experiments on telepathy, where holding the hand of the would-be percipient sometimes facilitates the transfer of an idea or scene, silently thought of by the other person.

W. F. Barrett, 1918

Introductory Note

By the Editor

The reports of sittings with Mrs. Osborne Leonard, in which Sir William Barrett (W.F.B.) purports to be the chief communicator, are given under his initials, and in conversation the sitter assumes the hypothesis that it is W. F. B. who speaks.

Readers who do not believe in the possibility of survival after death may find this method annoying, but is not any scientific hypothesis assumed to be true while we are testing its validity? On the other hand, it may be thought that messages purporting to come from the other side of death are of too private a nature to publish. This is true of many, and some of the most convincing scripts have had to be omitted on this account.

But others appear to have the intention of carrying conviction not only to the one to whom they were sent but also to others who will read them with an unbiased mind – conviction that death is but the opening of a new chapter in life's experience.

Sir William Barrett (W.F.B.), when studying the subject on Earth, had always realised that such conviction would only develop slowly. Writing in defence of the work of the Society for psychical research three years before he left us he said, 'Many perplexing problems still confront us, but we must remember how many centuries passed before physical science began to emerge from the disorderly mystery of ignorance into the orderly mystery of science.' The sittings from which the reported messages are taken have occurred every few months over a period of eleven years. They were not sought by me, although I had been interested in the subject of psychical research for a long time. On June 6, 1925, however, I received a letter from a member of the Society for Psychical Research previously unknown to me, enclosing notes taken at a sitting with Mrs. Leonard on June 5, 1925. (Sir William Barrett died on May 26, 1925.) The sitter, who was unknown to me, said in her letter:

> I had not the honour of your husband's acquaintance, but as a member of the S.P.R. I of course had often seen him and heard him speak. It is impossible to convey through the notes the vivid impression both my friend and I received that it was indeed Sir William manifesting.

Before quoting the messages received, it seems necessary to give a brief picture of his last day on Earth.

He was specially well and happy in the morning and spent most of it in writing and sending one or two letters to friends. He sent a postcard to our friend Mrs. Jervis, asking her to come to tea on the 28th inst.

He wanted to hear more about her recent experiences in America, and specially her views of the Piper circle – a little group of friends who had periodical sittings with Mrs. Piper, a celebrated medium, who has been investigated by the Society for Psychical Research.

A friend came to lunch with us (referred to in another sitting), after which he went to a Committee on Physical Phenomena at the S.P.R., over which he presided.

After tea he had an interview at which I was present, and at the end I went down to the front door with the visitor, and returned to find him lying sideways in an armchair beside a small table. I rushed to him, but he had ceased to breathe and no heartbeat could be felt. Restoratives were in vain.

The chief messages which concern W. F. B. in the notes of the sitting sent to me are as follows:

INTRODUCTORY NOTE

W. F. B. I want you to write to my wife just to say I came and that I am very well and happy. I want to give her my very fond love and say that I have sent a message from a place a very long way off – I can't get the name through here – it's from a quarter with which I had a very slight connection when I was here. The place I am speaking of is a long way away over the sea: the message will take some time to reach her; the journey would take perhaps a couple of weeks.

Control: He looks more like thirty years ago – no glasses, eyes bright and he can hear – he is so happy.

W. F. B. It is a great joy to me to hear again clearly and distinctly. Tell her my dear mother is with me and was with me at the moment I passed over. My mother stood by the table. I think she felt she must stand by me because she has told me she felt she must be with me all that day.

Control: Something to do with his leg is better; he draws a line from the knee upwards.

W. F. B. Thank you so much, thank you for allowing me to come, and don't forget to say what the medium told you about my looking well.

There were three statements in this message I felt to be important:

(1) That a message had been sent from overseas which might or might not be corroborated.

(2) That his mother 'stood by the table' at the moment of his passing. He died quite suddenly in an armchair with a small table at its side. He had always been devoted to his mother and she lived with him in Ireland till her death.

(3) That the pain in the thigh was better. For two days before his passing he had complained of pain in the left thigh. Neither the medium nor sitters could have had any knowledge of these trivial facts.

Stimulated by this message I went to a sitting with Mrs. Leonard in July 1925. At this sitting the 'message from oversea' was elaborated. He then said:

> The message was from America, not very north, rather towards the south. It was given to someone whose name began with P, a word of 5 or 7 letters. P is a prominent person connected with a group. I think it must come your way.

Some months later Mrs. Jervis told me she had received a letter from Mrs. Piper in Boston, U.S.A., about the middle of June, saying that Mrs. Piper had a message from Sir William Barrett: 'Tell Mrs. Jervis I am sorry I could not keep the appointment.' On the day that Mrs. Jervis read the obituary notice in The *Times* (May 27), she had received the postcard from my husband saying, 'Come to tea on Thursday and tell us more about America.' While in America Mrs. Jervis had visited the Piper circle. She was therefore the obvious link between Mrs. Piper and England. It seems worthwhile to record these early initial messages because so many think it is those on Earth who seek communication with their departed friends, and even regard it as a disturbance of their peace.

If personality survives death it is natural that those who have passed to a higher life should wish to comfort those with whom they had vital relationship on Earth, but this is not possible to all and there are many difficulties to be overcome.

An explanatory note may perhaps be given for those readers who have no experience of sitting with a trance medium.

The reader should note certain peculiarities in the form of communications purporting to emanate from W.F.B.; for example, a reference to someone or something with which both of us would be well acquainted may be introduced at a sitting in the form of a question.

It should be understood that this is the reaction of the control to the communicator's thought and should not be regarded as indicating that the communicator himself needs to ask any question about the matter.

INTRODUCTORY NOTE

Another point to be observed is that a quite definite reference to some personality or incident which W. F. B. would certainly know all about is introduced at the sitting in a roundabout way, as for example, in the statement about my recently deceased brother, which appears in the record of the sitting held on January 15, 1931. It will be seen from the notes the statement was made in spontaneous response to my own request audibly made to W. F. B. in my own home some little time before. A reader unfamiliar with the modus operandi of these communications might naturally wonder why a reference so clear and unmistakable should not have been differently initiated. Why should not W. F. B. have begun what he had to say by stating explicitly that he was in touch with my brother? The explanation is the same as what I have just said about the control asking a question. W. F. B. is apparently using the easiest method of conveying information to the control and having it impressed upon the medium's brain.

All experimenters in the field of psychical research are aware of facts of this kind and are accustomed to make due allowance for them.

See also p. 85, in the sitting March 9, 1929, where the direct voice of the communicator is contrasted with the interpretation of thought by the control (Feda).

The actual phrasing, therefore, in some places cannot be regarded word for word as that of the communicator himself, but as that of the control operating through the medium.

At times, however, the sitter is definitely impressed by the fact that the communicator is dictating his own message in the precise form in which he wishes it to be received. When this is so the style of delivery changes; the message is given slowly and with relevant pauses instead of quickly, as is the usual mode.

It occasionally happens that if the sitter interrupts by saying 'You mean so and so,' the communicator will reply, 'No, I mean what I have said.' When the sentence referred to is completed it is invariably found that the word insisted upon was the right word to convey his meaning.

See record of October 30, 1931.

Throughout the whole record as here given the abrupt transition from one subject to another is unavoidable, due to the elimination of personal and private affairs concerning ourselves or other people.

In the original script it is not so, as the ending of a private message may lead to the next subject.

The words of greeting at the beginning of each sitting and of farewell at the end are omitted in nearly every case.

Words heard in the direct voice apart from the medium are printed in italics.

CHAPTER 1

July 26, 1925
Leonard Sitting

W. F. B. I'm here. I sent messages by two ladies. I've tried to give you impressions about some material matters – about the house. I should like you to use my room. I have tried to impress this idea on you – I have not just thought of it today; use it for your consulting room. Is there something on the floor you want altered? I thought I saw you looking on the floor as though you wanted to change something – something about heat.

The idea of using his study as my consulting room had come to me quite suddenly one day when I was busy about other things. The idea came so vividly that I at once went down to the room to consider whether I could leave the room much as he used it and yet introduce the things essential for use as a professional room.

I searched round the wainscot near the floor – specially near the fireplace – to see whether he had arranged new electric stops, as I should need one in a position possible for my lamp.

F. E. B. What would you like me to do about the letters in your cash-box? Shall I destroy them?

W. F. B. Keep them for the present.
F. E. B. Do you want them destroyed ultimately?
W. F. B. Yes, but wait a little. Don't let anyone else have them. There is no ordinary material reason for keeping them, but some ideal. They are letters that were not written lately, but a long time ago – relics. I had thought of destroying them myself, but put it off.

These were letters written to him when he was a young man, including one from an old friend in time of trouble. The message accurately describes the letters, which are of a private nature.

F. E. B. Can you tell me anything of your passing?
W. F. B. When I passed over I had no pain at all: *at once* people were with me – my *mother* and father and others.
F. E. B. Did you know when I came back?
W. F. B. It was not knowing – being aware – not quite the same. I did not see or hear but felt. I was conscious of wanting you for a moment – a flash – I knew something was happening to me, and mentally I called out for you, so strongly I almost thought I had called out.
Then I felt you come back to me, but I was past seeing and hearing: it was very quick.
I remember trying to *turn sideways*: you may have noticed that when you came.
You hadn't gone for good. It was not my passing that called you: you had only *gone to come back again*.

I had left him to go down to the front door with a visitor with whom we had just had an interview, and when I came straight back to the drawing-room he was lying in the armchair and had ceased to breathe. He was lying sideways in the chair.
I rushed to him and felt his heart, but it had ceased to beat. He was apparently well when I left the room and had been unusually bright and active during the day.

INTRODUCTORY NOTE

There had been no possibility of Mrs. Leonard knowing these details.

F. E. B. Have you met Frederick Myers?
W. F. B. Myers? Of course I have. There were several friends to welcome me, but I was especially pleased to see Myers. I'm going to work with him.

Frederick Myers was a great friend. The expression 'of course' was very characteristic. Written down it sounds a little discourteous; it never did as he said it.

F. E. B. Do you want to tell me about your own papers? Are you satisfied with the arrangements I am making?
W. F. B. Yes. I don't want anyone else to do it.
F. E. B. What about your book *Visions of the Dying*?
W. F. B. You must write it. I will do it through you – no one else. Not by automatic writing, but I will impress you what to say. You finish it yourself; we'll do it together.

The collected material and some of the writing had been done, but the book was in quite an unfinished state.

W. F. B. It used to worry me because you worked so hard: it doesn't matter now because I know it's worth doing. Now I can help you more, so I'm not afraid of it. To feel full of vigour – able to do things – is wonderful.

I've started work with Myers. Needless to say I am specially working, trying to prove not only survival but the possibility of communicating.

F. E. B. Can I help you?
W.F.B. Yes – later on. I shall have to study it more.
You see, this is a new life for me. I have not yet become accustomed to my new life and to be able to use a body. It is an active life I'm glad to say. Stagnation was death to him.
W.F.B. I've met Crookes.

Sir William Crookes was an old friend. The following sentence was said in a deep voice, very slowly, and with emphasis, as though he were personally controlling the medium.

> W. F. B. There are two lives here: one I can tell you about and you can understand, and one I cannot tell you about till you come over.
> F. E. B. Which is the higher?
> W.F.B. The one I cannot explain.
> Oh, I *do* miss you. I can be with you, but I miss your knowing it. I miss the companionship. I have been with you, but it isn't quite the same. We can't talk, and it is the mutual understanding on interesting things that one misses.

This sentence was a surprise. The idea of those on the other side missing us had not occurred to me.

> F. E. B. Have you met any of my friends?
> W. F. B. Yes, but not many yet. I've been so full of meeting my own relatives and friends such as Myers.
> I have met A. She is a friend of yours. She was very pleased to hear the latest news of you.

My friend Ada Vachell, who appears frequently in subsequent sittings.

> W. F. B. A is rather an important friend. I was so pleased to be able to see her. A friend of yours, but she was a friend of mine too.

It is quite true that she was also his friend: when they first met they were friends at once, each appreciating the other.

> W. F. B. There is a B in connection with A – a place: write it.

The medium tried to write in the air but got the second letter more like a U.

INTRODUCTORY NOTE

W. F. B. said every time 'No, no, it's wrong; give a little twirl to the second letter.'

Ada Vachell lived in Bristol.

W. F. B. I have tried to give you a message wherever the power drew. We sometimes try people we don't know at all. In two or three places I have felt they had power – that stupid little man.
F. E. B. What stupid little man?
W. F. B. I went to the stupid little man with the slates – a long way off – I thought I'd see what he could do as he talked so much. You may get something later and remember.

A slate-writing medium had come to London a short time before with a great reputation. W. F. B. was anxious to have a sitting with him and had prepared what he felt would be foolproof precautions. We invited him to spend an evening before asking him for a sitting, but at the end of the evening W. F. B. said he had very little expectation of any good results as the man talked the whole evening about himself.

The medium did not give a sitting to anyone interested in psychical research during the visit to London, so the preparations were in vain.

W. F. B. There is a great deal I am going to do. You know how anxious I was to prove that even those people who have been sceptical all their lives, at the end know there is an afterlife even if too far gone to say so. *Many* of them have said so and that is what I wish to show in the script you've got.
The material I gathered did not refer only to those who have been believers or psychics. Some were, but some were not. I'm sure that the book will impress many people and help them. You know I had been working at it up to the last in order to prove it to them. I want them to know I was *active* and *sure* of my own mind, and could think things out up to the last. I always wanted to keep sane about the matter, to be balanced in regard to the whole subject.

(Here follows a long talk about intimate affairs concerning other people, which, though very evidential, is too private to publish.)

> W. F. B. Life is far more wonderful than I can ever tell you, beyond anything I ever hoped for; it exceeds all my expectations.

The control seemed here to disappear and a deeper voice spoke slowly and with great emphasis.
Having promised to end the sitting, after an hour I said 'Goodbye.'

> W. F. B. No, I'm coming with you. Do you remember I always wanted to go with you – even where I had no business to be?

This is typical of him. He often said when I was going to hospital, 'I wish I could come with you, but I know I've no business there.'

> W. F. B. *All* my love. My *undying* love.

So much has had to be eliminated from this sitting because of its private nature that its characteristic talk is lost.

I read the whole of it to an intimate friend of my husband, Philip Somerville-Large, and he exclaimed at the end, 'Why it's just like my old friend sitting here and talking to us – as he always did – turning to one subject after another, full of interest in them all.'

CHAPTER 2

September 20, 1925
Leonard Sitting

W. F. B. I have much to talk about and am very pleased with things generally.
About Ireland – something has happened to people I am interested in there – not you going there but something you've done – you've been helping people in Ireland. I was a little anxious about it, but am pleased now.
Two people from Ireland will be visiting England and I have a strong feeling that you'll be with them: that is apart from the other matter: two things made me think of Ireland; they are:

(*1*) The proposed visit of people in whom I'm interested and that you will see.
(2) The other matter you were reading about that pleases me now – not important.

The first reference to Ireland, together with 'something you were reading about,' refers to the Home of Rest, whose secretary had sent me a Report.
In a memorandum attached to his will W. F. B. said he would have liked to leave something to this institution but felt he could

not do so. I had been thinking of sending a donation to them in his name, but when I read the Report it seemed to me they would benefit more by my continuing his subscription, and this I had done a week before the sitting.

The morning after the sitting I had a letter from Philip Somerville-Large, an old friend who lived in Ireland with his brother, Canon Somerville-Large.

Both were close friends of W. F. B. In the letter he tells me he is coming to London within a day or two and would come and see me. The 'two people' are very closely linked, but only one came.

> W. F. B. You are going to use another room outside your house later on – not immediately – fairly soon; it will turn out later to be very important, that is your using a room in another house – a place where many people come and go.

This I could not understand at all at the time, but early in 1926 when I became Dean of the London (R. F. H.) School of Medicine for Women I had the Dean's room for my own use in that building, which is associated with important work for medical women.

> F. E. B. What are you doing in your new life?
> W. F. B. I have the greatest joy here – apart from my mother – the greatest joy and pleasure in my renewed friendship with Myers. I cannot tell you all the things we are learning together and I from him.
> It is linking up so many things I began on your side.
> It is a joy to hear easily again.
> Did I remind you last time that I had passed over near the date of what brought us together, the place where things were decided? [*Laughing*] That will give you something to think about.

This did indeed give me something to think about and I could not remember anything at all in my life, or at Buckstone Cottage, the place evidently referred to (we met there, became engaged there, and spent the first day or two of our wedding tour there), which coincided with the date of his death.

One day when very tired I fell asleep for a few minutes in the drawing-room and woke with the date May 26 before me and the little scene of my taking the cottage from the farmer and saying ' You've barely a month to quarter day. Can you get the repairs done by then?' It was exactly ten years to the day of his death.

> W. F. B. We've no idea of trying to find an elixir, but we have a feeling – more – on Myers' part it's knowledge – that the ugliness of physical death and the corruption of physical flesh is unnecessary: we have a feeling that it is not what was intended – it was not God's original intention that man should suffer the horrible breakdown of the physical organism that he does: the ugly trappings of death – the dispersal of the physical body – it's unnecessary and wrong. I feel it will be averted. I do not mean that man will live eternally, in consequence of the prolongation of life. I think he will live longer, but the transition to our planes will be gradual, not sudden.
> You remember Myers talking to us about the etheric body and its rate of vibrations. Myers and I feel that man can learn how to exist in and consciously use his etheric body in such a way that he will not function entirely in the physical, but will learn to use both bodies during his life on Earth, with the result that he will develop to a point when the physical body will gradually become etherealised and brought more into harmony with the etheric body: the vibrations of the so-called physical body will then become higher and a gradual transmutation will take place, so that the coarser physical body will in time be absorbed as it were by the etheric.
> F. E. B. Can we help towards this?
> W. F. B. Yes, in the line of spiritual consciousness: by realisation of the fact that there is a spiritual world: by aspiring to live daily, hourly, in thought, word and action according to the higher promptings of your own spiritual endowments. How Our Lord was an exponent of what Myers and I are

> trying to explain to you. He lived in such a way that He used spiritual forces as easily as He used material Forces through His material organism, and at death there was no physical corruption of His body. So you see *His body was not there*: it was transmuted into his spiritual etheric body. Through living in the most spiritual vibration He was able to raise the vibrations of the physical so that there was no body to dispose of at His death – or as we prefer to say, at His transition.

This was said slowly and very impressively. During the last few months of his life he was very interested in the question of whether there was really a disappearance of the body of Christ at His resurrection or whether the story of the soldiers stealing it was true. He thought it a subject for more careful research both from a Christian and a psychical point of view as well as historical. Now his statement seemed to imply 'This is the fact,' which explains and makes clear that the body was not there.

> W. F. B. We psychical researchers are often disposed to use the word transition, but judged by what happens to us at the present time on Earth, we cannot truthfully apply that word, or you would not have the physical body to bury or cremate. Our Lord's was in truth a transition – ours should be. We all know this over here, but we cannot all say it today. We don't get the conditions in which we can say it. A sitter is a very important factor.
> Some sitters might not be spiritually ready to help the communicator to give information of this kind.
> You want to know, and I want to tell, so the conditions are perfect. Out of thousands who communicate there may be only half a dozen who can speak of these things.

(Here follow very intimate communications, evidential to me alone – among them further details of his passing.)

INTRODUCTORY NOTE

> W. F. B. You know I've met a woman I was interested in who got extraordinary messages. The circumstances were so peculiar that I didn't want to be mixed up in them, but I was very interested and wanted to know more particulars. She got messages apparently from Crookes.
> F. E. B. Did they come from Crookes?

The last paper read by W. F. B. at the S.P.R. was on the subject of this particular mediumship, with a discussion of the question whether the messages did or did not come from Sir William Crookes. Hence my question.

> W. F. B. There were messages, but unfortunately they were augmented by her ability to read memories of things written on the atmosphere. I don't mean they were not genuine: some were given by Crookes – not all.
> Even while Crookes was giving them her subconscious mind elaborated them: not very interesting: I've met the lady: you know she's over here, but I'm glad now I didn't go into it too deeply on your side, it would have involved me in complications rendering it difficult to arrive at the truth. Here it's clear: there were some communications, augmented by the subconsciousness of the woman herself, but she was quite a wonderful medium though untrained and undeveloped.

The complications I did not understand at the time, but they were told to me a few weeks later by a friend of the lady who knows nothing of this sitting.

Here follows some discussion of physical phenomena and advice as to how to obtain the best results. It was the subject of discussion at the Committee at which he presided on the afternoon of the day of his death.

> F. E. B. How could I satisfy people of your identity, that it is really yourself who is talking with me?

It occurred to me that I had been absorbed in the naturalness of all our conversation, but if challenged to say how I knew it was W. F. B. himself who communicated, how could I prove it? Hence the question.

> W. F. B. It depends entirely on who asks.
> F. E. B. Well – say Sir Oliver Lodge.
> W. F. B. He would be most satisfied by the things I have told you of, that please and interest me most.
> Others would not be appealed to by what I have said to you: they would be more pleased if I said the wall-paper in the corner of my room was a little torn and now I feel a new paper. That would appeal to one type of mind. Lodge might be interested to hear it, but wouldn't want to come and talk about it: he would talk about the kind of thing we've been saying.

A month before his death he pointed out that the wallpaper in one corner of his room was torn. The room had been repapered.

He had a damaged door handle repaired recently, and was always very particular that repairs should be done at once when needed.

> W. F. B. Lodge is nearer the bigger, greater aspect of things than most.
> Now I want to say this: I was a good age when I passed over. Lodge is getting to a good age. Have you noticed we all become a little impatient of minor details – of so-called tests? We wanted to know not so much these little things – wall-paper, broken knobs on doors, book tests (though those were very interesting to me) – but we wanted to hear of the other land. It might be thought evidence of senile decay – has been by ignorant people – but it isn't so.
> Lodge is doing other things in which he needs all his physical, mental and creative powers.
> I think it is that as we draw nearer to the time when we too may journey to that little-known country our souls have already

INTRODUCTORY NOTE

taken wing and made exploratory journeys, acclimatising themselves as it were to the conditions to which they will soon belong. I feel sure that occurred in my case, and it is happening in Lodge's case. I don't mean he is going to come over soon – I feel and hope he has many years yet, but in the ordinary course of events he must be near that time.

Another type of mind would ask what I could do for them – could I prophesy something useful or help them? Another would say could I heal them? Everyone would ask me to prove myself in a different way.

I feel we must pursue the present lines of communication, but I realise that they are very limited.

Each of us is presented at birth with our own little private telephone. God has given each one of us a channel, a sense, by which we can reach those on the other side. You know, my dear, most children give evidence of psychic power, but it wears out in face of misunderstanding and antagonism and so many hard material facts which seem in opposition to their observation – many children are naturally quenched by it.

Soon – it may be months, it may be years – we may be able to develop again those lost faculties.

You have not lost them – you have them to a remarkable degree (but you must be more conscious of them – use them more: they are a little rusty: there is some stiffness in the working) – that is why you get so much from me. Later on you will be able to work them more, but you mustn't work too much at present.

I'm just as much with you. I have the better part because I can see you quite clearly but you can't see me. I *feel* you so distinctly that I don't need always to register impressions by looking, but I do at times.

Have you got the painting all finished? Some was done and some to be done later – light paint and washing in the big rooms. They could do with it, but I don't want to hurry you – I only mention it so that you may know I'm interested in it. I may want help to find you another servant – I feel some uncertainty in the household – the one who does rooms and things. I am particular about people in the house – it is not work only that matters, but themselves.

Of this I had no knowledge at the time, but the uncertainty had already arisen in the mind of a special maid on account of the failing health of her mother.

On September 21, 1925, the Rev. W. S. Irving had a sitting with Mrs. Leonard, at which his late wife was said to be the communicator. This sitting appears to have been used by W. F. B. to get through further proof of identity and of interest in his old home. The following message was given: (Communicator, Mrs. W. S. Irving.)

'Sir William Barrett invited me to get a book-test from his house, and he assured me it would be quite safe there, so I was not to be afraid that these tests would be spoilt in any way, because the Medium has never seen the house, and few people go into this particular room now at all, so he thought it would be a very safe place. Now, it's a room that he often used to sit in himself, the room he used mostly for sitting, and reading, and writing in. There is only one room that he cared to use in that way, so there is no mistaking it. As you go in you notice at once that there are a good many books there. Coming in the door there are books nearest to the first corner on the left hand side. I want you to go to the second shelf up, and take the 7th book from the left, to open it at page 11. It speaks on page 11 of "added strength, added power, greater opportunities," and he would like his wife to think of him in that way, and I would like you to think of me in that way.
'Within a span, on the outside of another book are words describing your calling, your profession, your work.'

The Rev. W. S. Irving reports:

INTRODUCTORY NOTE

'The day after the sitting I called at Sir William's house and Lady Barrett kindly helped me to verify the tests. I had not before met Lady Barrett, nor had I been inside this house.
'The first book indicated – 7th book from the left on the second shelf – was *The Mystic Way*. Page 11 deals with evolution. I found on that page the following sentences: – "Life has only one way of attaining any stage or state. She must grow to it. Hence the history of the Spirit is for us the history of growth." . . .
"The soul," says a great psychologist, "is no more absolute and unchangeable than the body." 'The second book – within a span – has its title on the outside – *Religion and Life*, by Elwood.'

I cannot help thinking, however, that the book tests were not the main evidence that it was desired to convey. At the end of the sitting the communicator said: 'Sir William told me a little while ago that he would be glad for me to try to get a test from his house, because he is there every day, and he feels it is just as much his house as when he was here in the physical body.
'Wait – there is one bit I've still got to give you from that room. It was, would you ask my wife if a picture has been moved from that room just lately, within the last day or two?'

I had taken down a picture recently and was reminded of the exact date of its removal; for my maid said, 'It was the last day of the Rose Show: you came in with an armful of roses and put them down to unhang the picture, and I took it upstairs the next day.' I had unhung the picture three days before the sitting, and my maid carried it upstairs two days before the sitting.

The date of the Irving sitting was Monday, September 21. The picture was taken down on September 18 and removed on the 19th.

CHAPTER 3

December 28, 1925
Leonard Sitting

After discussing some private affairs W. F. B. said:

Is one of the servants leaving? It's not that she is wanting to leave, but I feel she may have to. I may only get thoughts, but you'll hear about it even if she doesn't go.

Soon after I did hear about it in the following way. I had a sitting with a strange medium who has no knowledge of me or my affairs. She said, 'Who is Nelly?' I said, 'Why do you ask?' Answer, 'Because this man is calling "Nelly, Nelly" twice like that and says, "Nelly, do you remember?"'

Nelly was the maid who had always looked after W.F.B., and I therefore told her of what had been said and asked if she understood the meaning.

She said 'Yes – Sir William made me promise I would never leave you unless I was absolutely needed in my own home, and I have been rather troubled lately because I am afraid I shall have to go home.' She came back after a few minutes to say, 'Did he call

"Nelly, Nelly" twice like that?' I said, 'Yes, why do you ask?' She said, 'Because I always hear him call like that if you are not well. He did when you were in Italy and afterwards I heard you had been specially ill that day.' It was the Saturday before Easter, and I travelled from Santa Margharita to Rome that day in the initial stage of an attack of influenza.

Ultimately Nelly had to leave after the death of her mother to go home and keep house for her father.

> W. F. B. You are going to have very busy times in two or three directions – not only your work but mine.
> You are finishing the book. I am satisfied, not only with what is done but with what is being done.
> I have been helping about it – not only you, someone else. I have worked through you and the other.
> Something is being rubbed out at the very beginning and changed – it's an improvement, not a whole page, only a few words.
>
> F. E. B. Is it the title?
> W. F. B. Yes. It's better now for present purposes. You've had two before, first one, and you altered it to another, and now you've gone back to something talked of earlier – a reversion.

Quite true – the title of 'Visions of the Dying' had been changed twice since the last sitting to *Deathbed Visions*.

> W. F. B. It's going to be published in two places almost simultaneously and in one of these will be issued in two forms which I agree to and want you to approve too. That you will know later. I'm going to bring it about myself.

A few days later a letter from Mr. John Murray told of arrangements to publish in America and England. In America partly by sending pages printed in England and partly by having them printed in the U.S.A.

INTRODUCTORY NOTE

W. F. B. Have you had a little trouble in the ear that made you think how troublesome it would be to use an instrument as I did?

Yes – temporary deafness in one ear which reminded me of him.

W. F. B. We rely on sensing over here – something which is above reason, above ordinary logical thinking – something we get in flashes even in our Earth life: you and I and all of us depend for our best efforts on something we call inspiration or intuition – we only get it in flashes on Earth. I work by inspiration a good deal over here: I should like to have done it more than I did on Earth.
F. E. B. Tell us what your life now is like. How is it different from ours?
W. F. B. It is very different.

(*1*) Because there is freedom from physical suffering, from old age, from deterioration of any kind in the body – in fact I would say deterioration of any kind whatever.
(2) Everything here is progressive – stepping forwards and onwards, no going backwards, but undoubtedly the freedom from limitations of disease and decay puts one on a different working basis, leaving one more free to exercise those higher powers which undoubtedly we all possess even in our physical bodies. I have felt them: you have felt them.

F. E. B. How is life in detail different?
W. F. B. Well, I do not eat and drink: I am fed from without: that is to say I do not absorb nourishment through the mouth but through the pores of my skin. I assume that we do that to some extent on Earth: if not nourishment we absorb life-giving properties through the pores of the skin and the air we breathe.
I do live in a house – very like any house on Earth – some of the rooms are like the rooms at home. My mind needed the rooms

at home. We usually find ourselves in surroundings which become the habit or need of the mind during our latter years; we are not transplanted into entirely different surroundings.

Nature never transplants except into conditions as congenial as possible, and as like as possible to the conditions which prevailed in the first place. So here we find ourselves in very similar surroundings.

My house seems as if built of brick and stone and mortar and plaster. Your house seems as if built of brick and stone and mortar and plaster – but seems – for what is stone? What is brick? What is mortar? What is plaster? What were they in the embryonic stage? What will they be in a few years' time? Crudely speaking they are various kinds of dust held together and separated by a substance we call ether – the ether being animated by the force I was so interested in here, the life force. The actual substance in a brick is infinitesimal: the actual substance in a brick in my house is still more infinitesimal, because we depend much more than you do on moulding with ether rather than with atomic substance. You cannot mould with ether at will; we can. We work on ether directly – you work on atomic matter. It is the ether that is the important point, and the life force therein.

I wear clothes; we produce them by thought, but I did not produce my own clothes.

F. E. B. Who did?

W. F. B. A tailor. I might call him a producer of garments, but 'tailor' is a very good description. I am not clever or skilled in the production of suits, but others are, and they cannot do my work. Each one to his own trade for a certain time. My tailor may one day do my work, but for a considerable time after passing he is happier in his own.

I feel comfortable in a suit. Has anyone any objection to my having one? Yes, many will have, but they would have no objection to a white linen robe. There is the incongruity – the unreasonableness. I might have a white linen garment in which I should be most uncomfortable, but should be debarred

INTRODUCTORY NOTE

from clothing most suitable to me.

I am trying to find a working philosophy which will be useful and a guide to those on Earth who are trying to struggle to a definite plan or idea of life.

It seems to me from where I am most people are not even struggling but meandering on purposelessly, blindly, because they have no definite philosophy as to a starting point.

Myers and so many of us over here are trying to find ways and means of putting it to you on Earth in a simple way so that you can express it to the man in the street who needs it badly. We are so much happier than you, because even the lowest here is conscious of God. You wondered whether the teachings of Christianity were essential to the human race; the longer I am on this side the more convinced I am that it is so. Myers has been a great help to me. That is another thing, another difference: – on Earth it is difficult to meet, talk and work easily with those who could help one, but here if someone's help is necessary one has it.

I longed to be with Myers and talk to him – to know and see things I felt he could see and know.

I have met many, not only those passed over recently, but many thousands of years ago. I don't live with them or see them often, but it has been my privilege to meet them, to see them and to know that they exist. I have met someone of whom you have a sort of bust or picture at home.

F. E. B. I don't think so.

W. F. B. I know – it's of someone passed over long ago, in whom I was interested on your side, though never met; and I was delighted to meet him. He passed over before I could have met him. It's flat against the wall, with dark wood close to it.

F. E. B. What is the man doing?

W. F. B. He is in a much higher sphere; I only see him occasionally: he too is trying to help through a philosophy of – a kind of knowledge of – the spiritual life.

You've got a book about him too, one particular book. I also have that book where I am now. We can have books. I'm glad.

You have a copy. I want you to open it at page 87.
You'll find a good summary of one or two things I've talked to you about today in connection with the philosophy of life – especially concerning knowledge and intuition.

F. E. B. Where is that book?

W. F. B. It is both prose and verse – and blank verse, some dialogues and blank verse of a more miscellaneous character as well as what strictly one would call prose. H is on the book – word or name. He wasn't English or Scotch – and there are characters in different type – not ordinary letters – but be sure and look on page 87.

I think it will be helpful to you, will fit in with so much of what you are doing just now. I have a feeling that on the preceding page near the top is a suggestion of depression, worry, sad thoughts.

I was glad to turn to page 87 after.

But it seems extraordinary meeting this person.

Do you remember I was interested in him and his writings in connection with psychical research? You are not always near the picture, but you were near it recently. That put me in touch with it again. H. It is a picture not exactly made of plaster stuff. There are leaves in the picture.

In the book in the beginning a lot of numbers are mentioned.

It's brown. It won't be difficult to find the book.

A picture as described hangs over the fireplace in a room which I rarely entered at that time, but I had been there a few days before the sitting. The picture is a monochrome of a bas relief of the blind Bard, Homer, framed in dark oak. I found the book containing selections from the writings of Homer. It was a brown book which I had never opened before.

Page 87, however, did not give anything *re* a philosophy of life, though the book did contain prose, blank verse, dialogues, etc. I have so far looked in vain to find the book again, as it might give more exact references for this report.

INTRODUCTORY NOTE

> W. F. B. I have been trying to send you out cheerful, happy, strengthening thoughts. Helping you to make good resolutions more with regard to the mental life than merely physical – what you should think and feel more than what you should do. We can help you. We can't work out your development for you, but we can help you in the right direction: though we cannot force you to go in it, we can suggest.
> I see you doing an unusual amount of work in the near future: you've got to do it – now, almost at once.

On this day, December 28, 1925, Dame Louisa Aldrich-Blake, Dean of the London School of Medicine for Women, died, and early in 1926 I was invited to become Dean. It involved a great deal of new work, which necessitated my giving up various pieces of work which seemed to be less important.

> W. F. B. There's a lady with me – not my mother – she belongs more to you. She doesn't look old: what you would call in her prime. She doesn't feel ordinarily friendly. She wants to send her love to you. She knew you well here; you've done a lot together – sharing life together. B is the place.

Ada Vachell of Bristol.

> She wants to send a message to a man – with two syllables in his name. It starts with A like A in Ah! not A in Amy, and he was connected with B. Her brother Alfred Vachell, also connected with Bristol.
> F. E. B. Does she want to send a message?
> A. He feels me, he knows I'm living, but he doesn't understand it like you, but he feels and hopes I am near. It is someone I know very well: I want to send my love and want him to know that I am happy and active.

This very accurately represents his hope and belief in survival, but he would doubt communication.

A. There is a lady I have been worried about lately – she is not very well. I should like her to know I have been helping her. Tell her I liked the new little plant so much. It's green – not flowering, but with something growing on it. Not a berry, little knobs – something she's had recently. The little green knobs are hard.

Her friend M.G. who lived with her had not been well. I sent this message entirely ignorant of its meaning. She replied as follows: 'I understand the message. I had planted some grape fruit seeds in pots and they had grown into tiny trees covered with white blossoms at first, and subsequently fruit about the size of small green peas.

When watering them one day I was very conscious of Ada's presence and the plants were so lovely that I said aloud, "Do you like them, my woman?" This message seems to be the answer. – M.G.'

W. F. B. Have you looked for something to write with? I am giving it to you: I like you to have it.

I found his fountain pen when looking for something to write with.

W. F. B. Have you been doing something about blinds? Have you thought of arranging something different for some windows – darkening them?

I had asked my maid if she had put up darker curtains in the dining-room window; we were talking about them in the room.

W. F. B. I like to potter about and know about little things as well as big. I sometimes went into a room not for any special object when here, and I like to do it now. I come into rooms with you, and do not always sit still: I like to walk about taking notice of things.
Do you remember a discussion about ringing bells and not calling people? More like little arguments about it being

good policy or not. I'm not sure which was right, but I was reminded of it by something lately.

I had asked him not to call down messages as he passed the stairs to the kitchen because when the maid came up it often meant a long conversation outside a room where a doctor was seeing patients.

I had asked him to ring for the maid because then I knew the conversation would take place in his own room. A few days before the sitting, coming from his room, I did myself the thing I had deprecated.

> W. F. B. Especial love – *especial* love. I want specially today to say 'I'm coming' as it is somewhere special you are going, not home, and I am quite interested and pleased.

I was going to lunch in the country with a mutual friend.

CHAPTER 4

March 6, 1926
Leonard Sitting

W. F. B. I am pleased about the book. I see it going through now – things have got much further than when you were here last. It has all worked out very well. Something is happening about it almost at once – I am sure now that it's being printed – indeed it is an accomplished fact in a sense.

I am very pleased with the way it's been handled.

You've done it very well, but I feel grateful to a man too, and if I could I would like to thank him, for he seems to have caught my ideas of what was necessary. Don't let him misunderstand that. I don't detract from all his own ideas and the amount of work and thought he has brought to bear on it. I shouldn't like him to think I said he merely reflected thought, but it is exactly as I would have done it.

I am *very* pleased, *very* pleased.

Did you have to look up some very old matter for this book? You'll remember after – he took trouble to supply some information – looking up something in an old book of reference to things a long time ago – not in your memory.

Mr. A. Trethewy did give great help in the preparation of *Deathbed Visions*, both in verifying statements of reference, in preparing the index, and in most valuable advice.

A.V. (speaking of the change to another life.) They are the most satisfactory conditions that could be imagined, because so natural, one step at a time. I was glad and relieved to find that it was only one step that I was required to take when I moved from Earth to this condition. The surroundings in which I found myself are extremely like those on Earth, without ugliness, disease or pain.

W. F. B. It was different for me. It was all waiting for me very much as I had pictured – only much more wonderful. After I had rested for a little while, I felt like a boy on a holiday exploring a new wonderful place of which I had heard and conjectured and pictured, but which more than came up to my expectations.

F. E. B. Shall I like it when I come?

W. F. B. Yes, you will, you will: you like any place with possibilities. When you find yourself in a mental or physical cul-de-sac, you don't like it; but you'll love it here – you'll love it.

To me it's a perfect condition.

It is a great help when one comes over to be attuned to an idea of what it may be like even if one isn't quite sure of it.

F. E. B. Can you give me any help in my own work?

W. F. B. I am interested in cancer, and want to help you. It is in the alimentary canal that the mischief originates.

F. E. B. How can we prove it?

W. F. B. I am not talking of the *induced* disease, but that which grows naturally (I have to use that word though it is not good). You cannot judge by the induced disease. Cancer always has its origin in the alimentary canal. Clearly internal cleanliness is the one thing that is absolutely essential to prevent it: perfect digestion and elimination must be worked for. Diet has a great deal to do with it.

INTRODUCTORY NOTE

If we had the right diet from birth or early childhood we could not breed cancer.

F. E. B. What is the right diet?

W. F. B. Too much starchy food is the wrong one: a superabundance of stimulating food is bad. Over-stimulation produces irritation of a kind. Undoubtedly we need the juices with different salts found in fruit.

We need fruit and also grains, *e.g.* wheat, barley, oats – not in too refined a condition so that they produce a clogging starchy material, but a perfect wheaten or wholemeal bread: fresh lemons, apples, pears.

So many of the fruits disagree, or appear to disagree with people whose stomachs or intestines have for forty to sixty years been trained to the wrong diet and therefore rebel against the imposition of a right one.

If you were cramped and confined in a position in which you had to crouch down, you would be in terrible pain and discomfort when you were able to resume an upright natural position again. For a while the previous wrong position would appear preferable. That is how it seems to the stomach when you impose a correct diet. It may be too tired to respond at all. The thing to do is to teach people the right diet early in life.

F. E. B. Should meat be eaten?

W. F. B. That is just what I was going to say. I'm afraid of meat. I think we must learn to nourish our bodies with the right substitutes for it. As far as possible we should rely on vegetable food, supplemented by dairy produce, until we have educated our internal organs to live on plant life only. That might take several generations.

Nuts are stimulating, and where they cannot be taken whole they can be grated. Fruit juice would keep the alimentary canal clean.

With those who start to grow cancer, if they could be examined at an early stage there would be found to be a great deal of putrefactive material in the intestines.

F. E. B. What should be done?

W. F. B. *Washed out.* An intestinal disinfectant is needed and that should be used every day if cancer has begun. It would remove the cause of the trouble, and the disease would then be cut off from its supplies and would become a local and surface growth only.

I maintain that disease can only be a malignant one if there is a headquarter storehouse with a place from which toxin is supplied or material which creates sufficient force or life in the cancer enabling the growth to maintain its malignancy.

F. E. B. Would this treatment be any good in advanced disease?

W. F. B. It would alleviate but might not cure. It would alleviate and there would be a strong possibility of cure.

You have noticed in one or two rare cases of what appeared to be stubborn and malignant growth – it cures itself or disappears for no reason whatever as far as we can tell. It means something has shut off the supplies. These supplies were as the sap of a tree. Cut it off to a certain part or branch, and that part dies. That is what we've got to do with cancer. In a few years there will be no question about its origin. I know you will remember our little talk on the matter. It won't be disputed in a few years.

Constipation and even partial retention of impure matter is the curse of civilisation.

I believe meat, being as it is the principal part of diet, is at the bottom of a great deal of trouble.

I believe rheumatism, gout – in fact poisoning of any kind – has origin in this same canal – merely a different manifestation of the same system of poisoning. All the so-called cures that we have attempted with regard to cancer have attacked the manifestations and not the disease – i.e. not the seat of the trouble, which I consider is the disease.

Only good can come of trying this treatment on a very advanced case. I have a feeling that you'll have an opportunity of trying this – that you'll be able to soon.

Great care should be taken to prevent undue distension by injecting too great a quantity of liquid at a time – small quantities twice a day rather than one large injection given once.

I don't believe in a sudden change – rather a gradual change of diet.

I have spoken to a great many men who were interested in this subject on Earth and who have taken the trouble to use a faculty which would be best described as X-ray vision.

This is not guesswork on my part: they have been able to see the cause of the trouble and to watch the way it works out through the body.

We know the poisoning can be set up in a very acute way and yet the disease seems to be dormant for a long time, until some local irritation or some shock is given to any part of the body, and that draws the poison to the surface, makes it localise itself, and in that case it at once becomes active.

But if there were not the local shock or irritation the patient might live for years in the condition which we regard as *fairly well* – suffering from a mild form of rheumatism, indigestion, acidity, so many of the conditions which we accept as a natural part of our physical life. Absolute cleanliness in every way is the solution of most disease problems.

Another problem that interests me very much is the problem of heredity.

One of the penalties attached to the system of our wrong diet and wrong living is that we hand on a predisposition for these diseases to our children.

I have heard people on Earth say 'There is nothing in heredity' – but you must reckon with it. It can be overcome, but will be more difficult to overcome in the first generation than in the second and third.

Even if you give right diet at once to a child, you have inherited predisposition to disease to reckon with, but right diet will overcome it in time, and fortunately all disease (as all life does) has its rest periods – its dormant periods; though disease is the antithesis of life and the forces of nature, it is subject to the same rules and laws, and during the resting period is the time to tackle it. So often we disregard it in its dormant stage, which is its danger stage too for us, because in that condition it is gathering new strength with which to attack us later on. I still think people ought not to work too hard – on the same lines we've been talking about – because it produces congestion, mental and nervous, and congestion of any kind is to be avoided.

But I don't worry about you as much as I did, because I see one person can work hard and take it differently to another person, who does not work as hard, but is more conscious of the strenuousness of life.

It is the consciousness of it that makes the danger.

When you do become conscious it is Nature calling on you to stop. Some people go on longer before they reach the stage at which that must happen.

Also I feel that work that is productive is not so tiring as unproductive work. It is 'casting bread on the waters.'

A.V. Did I give you a letter last time?

H is the name of something I was very much connected with – Ho – not a hospital – it's nicer than a hospital – not kept up in any public way.

It is a nice place with a good deal of love in it.

W. F. B. Loving service. Ada can still help in those ways from where she is now.

These messages evidently refer to a Country Holiday Home which A.V. started in connection with the Guild of the Handicapped near Bristol.

A.V. Did you know I have a home this side – not for myself but for others to come to?

F. E. B. What is it for?

A.V. I'll use this term – people not yet quite sound in mind or body. There are people who come over who do not know how to use their minds and new bodies. Some have had long distressing illness, perhaps more of mind than body, and cannot learn to use their minds immediately: so we have homes in which they are helped by loving and sympathetic treatment and companionship to recover themselves entirely. That is what I love doing, only I can do it in an ideal way now, whereas there were difficulties on Earth.

April 9, 1926
Leonard Sitting

> W. F. B. I am glad to have a sitting near Easter, it has a definite message of hope for everyone. It is new life, new hope, new strength, and it is right that Easter should have come in the spring because the two harmonise so well with each other.
> This Easter I have specially tried to bring to you all this strength and peace, and I believe I have been to some extent successful in bringing these conditions round you. I am bringing you strength and peace specially this Easter, because there is such a great deal to do.
> I have been a great deal with you lately and I think you have known it. I want to go on with my investigations, not just psychical research, but into your work. When on Earth I took a great interest in your work though it was not my own, and if younger I would have taken a still greater interest in it. But I find I can do even more than I thought possible.

Every week he used to read the *British Medical Journal* and the *Lancet* to give me a digest of them in case I should miss any article of importance.

> W. F. B. I am more than ever convinced that on the lines I indicated to you is to be found, I won't say the cure but the correct preventive measures to be taken against cancer, and certainly great alleviation may be obtained through the diet and internal cleanliness.

There is something I want to get through with regard to germ theory – amplification – referring to the external gases given off in so-called infectious diseases – it is most important if only I can give it.

The harmful condition given off by an infected person is not only due to bacteria but to the gases in which bacteria live and infect and poison. I wish to say the harm is not in the germ but in its aura.

We have noticed that the easiest way to become infected is to breathe in, to take in the bacteria.

But in order that it should infect one, that is to make certain that one would be infected, one would have to take in not only the bacteria but a certain amount of the gas – the bacteria cannot live except in the gas. Bacteria of any kind must have their own gas to live in. If the gas is a harmful one the bacteria become harmful bacteria; if it is a good one they become beneficent. You see we are all giving off some kind of gas all day long, all night; every part of us gives off this gas or ether, whichever you like to call it. A healthy part of the body gives off a different gas from an unhealthy or diseased part. This gas of course is quite invisible; that is, it is not possible to locate it at present; but it will be. In a very short time indeed we shall go a step further and not only locate the germ as we do now, but locate the aura of the germ. That is all I can say about it at the moment.

The present condition, whatever it may be, will not permit me to say all I wish to say on a definite subject; but, for the time being, it is as though I were using up a certain amount of material, and then I have to change over and use a new material. I have other interesting things to say about it later on. But what I specially wish to say at the moment is this: We shall have opposition in certain quarters to this idea, but in a comparatively short time, while you are still here, you will find this theory is being accepted; other people will say they have discovered it, but it will be on the lines I have just indicated. Ada sends her love. She says the home is getting on very well, not the Earth one, the one she has got now. She says you have been in it with her. You have seen it – not in your sleep – not quite the right way of saying it – but you have been out of your body and have seen the home and approve of it.

Do you know, when she was here she was interested in a Home that was not quite in London, but more outside where there are fields? Because she is showing me a picture of the home she has now, and says it is like the home she has seen and it is not one of those in London but in the country – flowers and trees all round. Cannot see the water but she says it is there, she says there was water near, not the sea, just a bit of inland water quite near, and she believes that you could find out about it. She knew it very well, the water, only a short walk from the house itself.

I thought this could not be so, but on enquiry I find that from one corner of the garden of the Guild House, Churchill, or from an adjoining field water as described can be seen.

W. F. B. She says not only for children on the other side, she has grown-ups there too, and she says she takes them in when they come over; they have been suffering and unhappy for a long time and they have been treated there, not because they have got the conditions now over there, but the habit of thought that has been produced through the condition they have had on Earth; that is what has been eliminated, and she says that is what her home is for.

But I feel she has great sympathy with all kinds of trouble. That was the work she was most fitted for: it was the mental help she gave them, not only physical help – surroundings.

There are two people you have met lately, since you were here last, who have interested me and taken me back to the time when I was on Earth.

Do you remember a long time ago meeting the Medium in a street in a country place on an island? You were reminded of that place a little while ago, and it made me remember about seeing her there. It is not important but to get the reminder with you.

I had been seeing Louis and Olive de Sibour in town. When we were staying with them in Shanklin we did one day meet Mrs. Leonard and her friends out walking.

> W. F. B. I think that looking back I had a long life of remarkable happiness, and especially at the period at which most people are going down hill and getting depressed. I was remarkably happy, and I did like little jokes and hope it did not worry you. There was a joke about a man I met in the road, one about a stupid man in a road.

A pedestrian asked a man sitting on the roadside how long it would take him to reach Bristol. 'Go on,' said the man. He asked again, and again the man said, 'Go on.' He went on, saying, 'Silly idiot.'
'It will take you half an hour,' called the man.
'Why could you not say that before?' asked the pedestrian.
'Because I had to see how fast you walked,' was the reply.

> W. F. B. I am going now. I have the idea of a dog, a dog I am taking care of for you. It passed over. You have had it. I am keeping it for you; it is quite a small dog, but it is all right. I cannot get his name through; I will bring him again. I was very pleased to find animals lived on this side. Only animals that loved us.

See reference: Mrs. Barkel, March 9, 1929.

CHAPTER 5

August 9, 1926
Leonard Sitting

W. F. B. You mustn't sign that paper of hers – the woman's.
F. E. B. Do you mean the medium's?
W. F. B. Yes, you mustn't sign the paper she has on the table for you. I have certain things and work I want to do with you, and it will prevent my doing these more important things if you put your name to such a paper. Of course you must do as you like about it, but I hope you will not do it.
F. E. B. Of course I will not sign it if you do not wish me to.
W. F. B. I most certainly do not wish you to sign it. I hope to help and influence people through you, but many of them would be prejudiced against you in advance.
F. E. B. I won't sign it if you don't want it.
W.F.B. I don't want it. I am not against anyone affirming what they believe, but your profession – I want to help you in that too, and it would spoil it if you gave your name now to such a thing.

Some time before this sitting Mrs. Leonard sent me a proposed foreword to her book which she asked me to sign. Sir Oliver Lodge had promised to do so too. In it was stated that 'We are convinced that through Mrs. Leonard we have been put in communication with our departed friends.' I wrote and said that she was probably asking my signature as a scientific woman and I had not sufficient evidence to prove to enquirers what was claimed: I was quite willing to say that I had confidence in her bona fides.

Mrs. Leonard had replied that Sir Oliver also did not like the foreword and was going to rewrite it.

At the end of this very emphatic advice not to sign the paper the sitting continued.

At the end, when Mrs. Leonard came out of trance she took a paper from the table and said, 'This is the foreword Sir Oliver has written; I am sure you will be willing to sign this.' I felt the only course was to tell her just what had been said at the sitting.

She looked very disappointed, but after a few moments' silence she said, 'Well, I know I should not do anything myself if I had such a message from the other side, so I cannot ask you to do it; but I *am* sorry.'

> W. F. B. I am going back to what I was talking about last time. I felt the majority of people would say 'Nonsense, science has disproved it.' I was talking of poisonous or destructive gases, and specially in relation to various bacteria.
>
> In a few years – while you are still here – it will be an established fact, viz. that bacteria are not malignant except for the gases.
>
> I do not want to put the bacteria into one class – there are different kinds and types, but those are only differences of form, not one would be malignant if it were not for these gases. I believe there is extreme similarity between the form, shape and type of bacteria which belong to entirely different diseases, yet the bacteria prove to be very similar.
>
> Now you have rays that are capable of breaking up the gas – but some of the rays as you have them now cannot reach in all cases the region or locality of the gas. We must either find a way of intensifying the rays so that they will have

greater powers of penetration, or we must find some way of inducing the gas to come to the surface so that we can attack it with the rays.

I think we can do one or both soon. It is some kind of ray – probably the same already discovered, but an adjustment is necessary. It seems to me everything is a matter of adjustment. We don't want new powers, but to learn how to adjust those we already have. Electricity in its early stages was used in a crude elementary way – it was adjusted crudely: electricity hasn't improved in itself, but we have learnt how to manipulate and adjust it. Steam hasn't improved or altered in any way, but we have learnt how to adjust it.

F. E. B. Have you seen a friend of mine who passed over lately?

A medical friend of mine was knocked down by a motor car and died in a few minutes before she could be taken to hospital. The impression given of her is true to life.

W. F. B. Yes, it was sudden – very unexpected as far as Earth could see, but not unexpected from our side.
F. E. B. Have you seen her?
W. F. B. Yes, but it was not an ordinary accident, it was *meant* from our side – inevitable – something that was *allowed* to happen. It seemed to Earth like a tragedy, but I feel, and she too now, that she had to go over for two reasons:

(1) To prevent her doing something on Earth.
(2) To enable her to work on this side and do things here far more completely and happily than she could on Earth.

She was not altogether happy on Earth, though no one would know it.
She is conscious and knows what has happened.
She has a mind alert to things, quickly open to the fact that she has passed over and what happened and she is content.

She might easily have felt rebellious, for her life was not finished as she wished.
She might have done so much more for other people.
It seems so hard – but she doesn't feel that.
She is very interested but has not had time to learn everything all at once, but she is awake and trying to understand.
I haven't told her I would be talking to you today for a special reason – I didn't want her to come with me till she was more accustomed to things. I am afraid it would wake up all sorts of problems in her mind which it is best for her to put on one side for the present, because now she is at peace and happy and interested and not too much in touch with Earth conditions which occurred in connection with her passing.
Was she worried just immediately before passing? Because they are specially guarding her from anything that might bring back to her the condition of *shock – a blow* – I don't like the word but it conveys the idea.
Something went wrong – delay – a little before it really happened, which didn't help matters when it did happen. Do you know if something was delayed or held up a bit?

She was said to hesitate in the road.

Looked at from Earth point of view it seemed a terrible – a lamentable thing, but I want to tell you that in some curious way *it was meant to be – it was meant to be.*

CHAPTER 6

February 8, 1927
Leonard Sitting

I had been asked by Archdeacon Talbot (later Dean of Rochester) to book a sitting for him with Mrs. Leonard if possible as his son Michael had died recently and he hoped he might get in touch with him. I had succeeded in booking one for the week following February 8, and before coming to the sitting here recorded I had asked at home that if possible W. F. B. would tell me anything he could about Michael, who I explained was well known to Ada Vachell.

It may seem curious that in the midst of speaking of Michael Talbot another subject is introduced: it seems to be necessary that the sitter's mind should be diverted from a subject if the communicator is to have a chance of discussing it in his own way without interference of preconceived ideas. In this sitting, after giving further information about the lady who was killed in a motor accident and the man who committed suicide, he reintroduces the subject of Michael – A.'s friend.

F. E. B. Does Ada know about a young friend of hers recently passed over?
W. F. B. Yes, she does.
F. E. B. And is she going to help?

W. F. B. She has already helped, not only when he passed over but often here.
F. E. B. Will his friends be convinced that he is alive?
W. F. B. They may not be convinced suddenly, it will take time.
F. E. B. Will you be able to help?
W. F. B. I shall try my very best.
F. E. B. Do you know whom I mean?
W. F. B. I shall come back to it, shall refer to it later in the sitting. But A. has got the friend.

(Here follow further notes about the friend who was killed in a motor accident.)

F. E. B. What about the other you told me of at a previous sitting?

This question refers to a friend who committed suicide.

W. F. B. Do you mean the man who went over suddenly? I have been helping him: he is not quite so happy as the lady. He was not, and could not be, but he has been working things out lately. He was not a bad man; he is not that, but there was a certain amount (I have to put it this way) of lack of consideration with regard to other people's feelings that he has got to work out on the other side; it was not that he would be unkind if he knew it – he would not be – but he lacked the ability to see the thing that he thought was right from the other person's point of view; and on the other side he has had great help to rise above himself. You rise above yourself and find your higher self, and that is what this man had to do. You know the younger one that passed over lately, the one that A. was a friend to – he went over rather quickly.

Here the subject of Michael Talbot was introduced voluntarily by the communicator, a method which usually gives the best results.

INTRODUCTORY NOTE

W. F. B. He did not know he was going, but had to have help to get over the sense of surprise and shock. He has got over it and is perfectly happy, but there are two people on Earth that he is desperately wanting to comfort and he will get through. I am not speaking just of sittings, *but making them feel him, just at home; that is how I feel he will do it and it is the best way.*

Clearly his parents, Archdeacon and Mrs. Talbot.

W. F. B. Is there a man belonging to him who has not been well on Earth? Because he has been rather worried about a man on the Earth, who has been down and dull – not only grief but poor physical condition.

His father was very run down in health at the time.

W. F. B. There are really three people on Earth who are interested – but two particularly, father and mother. The third one does not matter so much; the name begins with J.

His brother, but older than himself and they were not much together.

Control: A name beginning with B comes up while I am talking about him.

Archdeacon Talbot was at that time Canon of Bristol.

W. F. B. Do you know a name beginning with W connected with him? Perhaps you would not know, but people belonging to him on Earth might – a name he was thinking about just before he passed over, not a short name, two or three syllables beginning with W.

The explanations that follow these questions were given by his parents. I had no clue to any of them at the time of the sitting.

They had stayed recently near Watergate Bay and Newquay; he loved the sea and had talked much of it during his illness.

W. F. B. Will you ask them whether he would have been thinking of chains before he passed over – you would not know. I feel sure they will understand that, because he says 'the chains are gone.'

In a much later sitting with his mother Michael explained how all his reserve went after his passing: 'Don't you remember in the first or second sitting I said the chains were off, the barriers were down; that helped Father more than anything else.'

W. F. B. You know the young man we have been speaking of had been active and energetic, full of life. I do not think he thought he would pass over so young.
There has been a youngish man, but older than this one, who passed over and was very pleased to welcome him as well as A. I had better say that again because they will know who it is. A man, a youngish man, who came to meet him, who passed over earlier. His name begins with R, and he was so pleased to see him. Someone his people knew, but belonged to a few years ago, not lately.

A friend, Richardson, who was killed in the war. This description was recognised at once by his parents.

W. F. B. Do you know if they had been talking about sea trips or ships before he passed over? Something seemed to be in his mind about the sea and ships. It is all the better really if you do not know.

He was speaking of Newquay, the sea, and ships, just before he died, and a picture of ships was hung before his bed at his request.

W. F. B. There is someone else who has helped him very much who had passed over. Someone who came to meet the young

> man when he passed over. A woman, rather dark in colour, who would have been about 65 to 70 when she passed over; her hair had turned grey, but she still had dark eyebrows, smooth hair parted in the centre, a face more long than round, thin a little in the cheeks, rather good features, nose is rather straight, showing the bridge just a very little. She is related to the one who has just come over lately. You would not know her, but the other people would, the two elderly people, they would know her; she is connected with them.
> Perhaps you could guess, but you had better tell them just what I say. She is a very good woman, helping him and bringing him up over there as well as A. A. is helping a good deal.

This description was recognised as applying to Michael's aunt, Miss Talbot, who was related therefore to the two elderly people, his parents.

I knew nothing of any of these details, but wrote them down and read them to Archdeacon Talbot, who recognised them one by one as I read.

> W. F. B. A. is very happy, always happy, quite satisfied with everything round her. Just like her, because she made the best of everything on Earth. She did not always have everything she wanted, but used to try to help everybody. She is still helping children, not her children, lots of children – helping everybody it amounts to.
> I never knew anyone so courageous, so selfless; she is so strong and she is gentle, she is both. She never thought of herself when she was here, always trying to think what was best for others, for other people round her.
> You were thinking of her very much indeed a few days ago and A. felt it and was close to you.
> F. E. B. Does she know why she was close?
> W. F. B. She knew you were thinking of her, missing her and yet feeling happy about her. Can you remember you were looking at something reminding you of her?

F. E. B. Does she know where I was?

W. F. B. It was where you were in a way that was bringing her round you, bringing up thoughts of her; but I cannot help thinking there was something particular that you looked at that made you think of her. I keep getting the idea of wood, something to do with wood that she was speaking of; perhaps I shall get it later. It was reminding you (not just now) of her, of her conditions on Earth. Yes, wait a minute, she says you were not thinking just of her only, but it was of her work that you were being reminded.

The week before I was at a public dinner in the room in Bristol where Ada and I sometimes used to lunch together and where we first planned to take our factory girls with us for country holidays. All the development in her work, from factory girls' holidays planned in that room to the development of her work for the cripples in Bristol, also discussed there, came back to me. I recognised the wood panelling in the corner of the room where our lunch table used to be, and pointed it out to the chairman at the dinner, who knew Ada and her work.

F. E. B. What do you think of all that people say is going to happen this year, wars, etc.?

W. F. B. Certain things undoubtedly will happen, but as usual they are exaggerated. Things though have been happening, atmospherical things chiefly. But I do not see great war, no great world war, and no plagues wiping out the whole populace. But the inevitable effect of things that have happened in the past is an extraordinary disturbance of the elements.

I will tell you now because you can look back later on and see what I said. There will be extraordinary storms, extraordinary storms.

F. E. B. Soon – this year?

W. F. B. Yes, this year, extraordinarily violent storms, earthquakes, tidal waves. There always are some, but they will be more frequent. I want you to put that down because you will hear of it.

INTRODUCTORY NOTE

On January 7, 1928, the Thames broke through the Millbank Embankment. See also the Press late in 1927 for corroboration of unusual storms, etc.

W. F. B. But wherever the right thought is held there will be protection; I know that, and one holding the right thought can protect another; and of course there have been unusual storms in the last year, and there will be more unusual ones now, but it is a hopeful sign.
F. E. B. Of what?
W.F.B. Of our breaking through.
F. E. B. How are you going to break through?
W. F. B. I feel we shall break through, that we shall in some way adjust ourselves to you and you will adjust yourselves to us, probably a little of both.
F. E. B. So we can talk to each other?
W. F. B. Yes, yes. I feel that this will come in your time; the move forward from your side combined with the move on our side – that is making the congestion.
It is the pressure from both sides that is making all these disturbances; where there is this pressure there is bound to be congestion; all the elements are electric and magnetic, and where you get too much compression there must be congestion. Do you know I am very interested in dreams? I do not mean ordinary dreams, but in the possibility of going to the other side during sleep. I am always hoping that you may do that, and that you may remember clearly having seen me. No, you have not done it yet, but I am always hoping that you will.
F. E. B. Are you making any plans to prove things to people this side?
W. F. B. Yes, that is what I am busily working at.
F. E. B. Can we do anything to help?
W. F. B. You cannot help, you cannot do more than you have done. We are waiting till these storms, these disturbances are over, then we shall get in more.
It is a case of tuning in better.

The blood has a vibration of its own, but also thought has a vibration of its own, a very important one: when we can tune our thoughts and our senses to the same vibration we shall be in communication.

Sound vibrates at a certain rate, but light is quicker than sound, much more rapid, and we have to learn on the Earth to tune in, to adjust ourselves to different vibrations. It may be possible that one person can tune in to a certain rate and not another, but this will be understood and will be catered for. People will be taught adjustment. They are taught mental control now; later they will be taught vibration control. We vibrate much more rapidly than you. It is easier in some ways for us to slow down to you than for you to vibrate quickly to us. Directly you try you get strain; there is tremendous strain in vibrating more rapidly than is natural to you. In exaltation and in moments of great danger one would vibrate more rapidly, and a time or period of danger or strain extended too long produces what we call a breakdown, the strings become too taut.

F. E. B. Does that produce what you call a mental breakdown?

W. F. B. It does.

F. E. B. Do psychic things produce that?

W. F. B. They could most certainly. If you were to live in a psychic strain too much you would break down under it.

F. E. B. So that people cannot do more than a certain amount?

W. F. B. No, they must not. I do not agree that psychic development causes insanity, but doing too much of it might result in causing a breakdown. If you run you feel your heart going and you get out of breath.

You would not be surprised if you collapsed. That is a state of strain undergone too long. And so it would be if anyone were too continuously in a psychic strain. But it helped me over things, and I feel it will be the same with you.

Sometimes I lose some memory of things from coming here; I know it in my own state but not here.

In dreams you do not know everything, you only get parts in a dream. A sitting is similar; when I go back to the spirit

INTRODUCTORY NOTE

world after a sitting like this I know I have not got everything through that I wanted to say.

That is due to my mind separating again, the consciousness separating again. In the Earth body we have the separation of subconscious and conscious. Consciousness only holds a certain number of memories at a time. When we pass over they join, – make a complete mind that knows and remembers everything, but when one comes here to a sitting the limitation of the physical sphere affects one's mind, and only a portion of one's mind can function for the time being. When I withdraw from this condition one's whole mind becomes again both subconscious and conscious; my subconscious mind encloses my conscious one and I become whole again mentally. I think that accounts for many people getting the idea (and it is wrong in one way and right in another) that it is bad for them to try to communicate, because certain people have sensed that there is limitation in communicating with another plane of existence and they have exaggerated it. I cannot come with and as my whole self, I cannot.

F. E. B. Why is that?

W. F. B. Because I have a fourth dimensional self which cannot make its fourth dimension exactly the same as the third. The fourth dimension is an extension – that is not the right way of saying it, but the only way I can say it. It is like measuring a third dimension by its square feet instead of by its cubic feet; that is very much the difference between third and fourth dimension; and there is no doubt about it I have left something of myself outside which rejoins me directly I put myself into the condition in which I readjust myself.

F. E. B. Are you alone or are there others here?

W. F. B. A. has been, but now I am alone. I like to come alone except for A. I never mind A. You know that occasionally Myers has been with me, but he has not been today. But I like to come just by myself; I know I get messages through more unadulterated, more exactly what I want to say.

F. E. B. Have you spoken to Olive?

W. F. B. I have – another man was with me when I spoke to Olive.

F. E. B. Who was the other man? Was he able to speak himself?

W. F. B. A little, not much – rather disappointed with his part of it. But there is another name beginning with P, a short name, something mixed up with Olive – it is about that the young man wanted to speak.

A few weeks before this sitting W.F.B.'s niece had gone anonymously to a medium, Mrs. Brittain. She came to see me immediately after to tell of what occurred.

At first she had been disappointed and was inclined to leave, regarding the whole thing as a fraud, when a very accurate description of her late husband was given as standing near her. She asked his name, and the medium said she could not make out what he said; was it Henry? Charles? etc. Again complete distrust nearly made the sitter leave, when she was arrested by a description of her uncle, W. F. B. 'Well, ask him to tell his name,' she said incredulously.

The medium replied, 'He is laughing at you, and says, "Tell her Uncle Willie sends his love."' Uncle Willie was the name she called him and their interviews together were always very merry.

The medium continued: 'He says, "When I have completed my researches on ectoplasm Chris (Chris was her husband's name) will be able to speak to you himself direct. He wants to tell you he has his boy about fourteen years old with him; he is very fond of him; but he loves Phyllis and Joy just as much as ever."' The medium said, 'This boy looks as though he has always lived in the spirit world. He could only have lived an hour or two on Earth.' Fourteen years before a son had been born to them who only lived an hour. Phyllis and Joy were their two girls, one older, the other younger, than the boy. After further messages had been given W. F. B. said very emphatically, 'Chris wants me to say be sure to tell Phyllis "Daddy did heal his little girl's finger."' Six years before this sitting – shortly after the death of 'Chris,' when W. F. B. was still with us – Phyllis was staying with her mother in the north of England when she had her finger badly crushed in a door. She was then only nine years old; she was put to bed to recover from the shock, and her mother was reading to her in the afternoon. Suddenly the child said, 'Oh, Mummy, there is a cloud or something coming out of the wall – it's moving towards the fireplace. Why, it's *Daddy*! He is in his grey suit and he is smiling at me.' Olive told W. F. B. of this episode at the time, and he was very interested, for he said it was rare to hear of a vision seen by so young a child and reported in words so suggestive of the way materialisations have been described in the séance room.

This child had no knowledge of any psychic happenings.

It seemed to me therefore very evidential that he should be anxious for the message referring to this event to be given.

I did not realise, however, the full import of the message till six years later, when Phyllis, then aged twenty-one, was staying with me in London.

She was speaking of her visit north years before and said, 'It was when I saw Daddy.' I replied, 'Weren't you very interested by the message he sent you?' She said, 'What message? I've never heard of any message.' I told her of the sitting her mother had six years before as related above, and especially the emphasis on the message to her.

She said, 'Of course you know what did happen to my finger?' I said, 'No; tell me.' She said, 'It was all discoloured you know, and very painful; they thought the nail would have to be taken off, but after I had seen Daddy, when Mummy looked at the finger it was quite the normal colour, and not at all painful, so I got up, and that was all.'

> F. E. B. Have I prevented you from giving any information by asking questions?
> W. F. B. I like questions. I like a mixture, sometimes talking myself and sometimes answering questions.
> F. E. B. You do not prefer my asking questions at the end?
> W. F. B. No, because sometimes the power goes and then it is too late. I feel it is going now.

August 17, 1927
Leonard Sitting

> F. E. B. Can you tell me anything of the future – next year?
> W. F. B. I can never say what will happen at a definite time. Some people think the end of the world will come next year. I do not. I think it is a pernicious idea and will do a great deal of harm: I do not think the end of the world is anywhere near, but there will be great changes.
> I told you of the great atmospheric conditions that have happened, and will – even this autumn. There will be extraordinary storms and floods in England, in the world generally – but here too. Of course there will not be earthquakes here, but there will be in other parts for some time I am afraid.

Reference to the Press of the late months of 1927 confirms this. It was the year of floods in London.

> W. F. B. This does not mean there will be no summer next year; it might be a splendid summer.

The summer of 1928 was a glorious summer.

> W. F. B. England on the whole is most fortunate, but will experience phenomenal conditions. We are very sensitive to atmospheric conditions when we come near your plane. These conditions are leading to something – revelations.
> F. E. B. To everyone?
> W. F. B. No, to those ready for them and receptive – mentally prepared. This has always been predicted. It is drawing near – it will come, I think, in your time and I shall be doing something with and through you, though I don't know what it is yet.

CHAPTER 7

September 26, 1927
Leonard Sitting

The record which now follows might seem to be very mixed and incoherent to anyone unacquainted with sittings with Mrs. Leonard if no prior explanation were offered.

It began like many before with welcome, the foretelling of my association with another institution for sick people; alterations to be done to my country cottage, and from that to coming world changes and the revelations from the world of spirit which he had previously foretold.

Into this came suddenly the name 'Florrie' in his own voice, apart from what was being said through the Control. It was a name by which I had been called by many in my childhood, but never used by him; hence a sudden acute doubt arose in my mind of his being really the communicating entity, and my request for some proof to be given that it was really my husband speaking.

He asked me to leave it to him and carry on the conversation as before.

I readily agreed, for I remembered a sitting to which we had come together before his own passing when Frederick Myers was the communicator and was discussing the power by which communication became possible. He called it for convenience X power and said it was more allied to Earth conditions than to theirs, and therefore if the sitters or the mediums willed what should be done with it, the communicator was quite powerless to do anything.

I remember asking how we could get the subject introduced that we wished to discuss or hear about, and he said we could ask it at home a day or two before the sitting by thought or by writing it down, or if we wished to be very emphatic, by speaking our request aloud in our own room.

Hence I was content to go on recording the sitting in the ordinary way; and it will be observed how after gradual testing of his power to speak and also to control what was said, successive proofs were given of his identity introduced by the spoken words *'my whistle,' 'Edward,' 'George'* (answer to a request made in my room the night before); *'tin box,' 'patch.'* The notes to these explain their relevance; but the tin box test needs some further note, for without the greatest care on the part of the communicator the test might so easily have seemed false. When I first asked the question, was it cash or manuscript box, the reply was 'No, much smaller, you've touched it recently,' which made me think it was a small tin box containing a few glass tubes of tabloids which belonged to him and he always took away with him. For the first time I had used this box myself a week or two before, and hence I knew I had touched it; so I asked, 'Did you take it away with you?' Reply: 'I kept it secreted on my person.' Question: 'What did you use it for?' expecting the reply, 'To carry my medicines,' but instead the Control said, 'He isn't saying anything, but he is showing me a very little box [acting the movement of lifting the cover], something round in it – he takes one out and puts it in his mouth.' Then he said, 'Sometimes when going visiting I was almost in a panic for fear I had left them at home.' I was now quite sure he alluded to a very small box of nitro-glycerine tablets which he always carried on his person, and I said, 'I ought always to have remembered them for you.' He replied, 'You used to ask me sometimes if I had them.' I then remembered that he had said I had touched it recently, and I had not seen one of his boxes since he went, and thought someone had thrown them away. So I said, 'I have not touched that box,' to which he replied, 'You have,

INTRODUCTORY NOTE

but do not trouble about it now, I'll make you remember at the right time.' When entering my bedroom a day or two later I remembered that recently I looked in my medicine cupboard for menthol tablets for a friend, and found that my maid had put all the little tin boxes in a pile on one side. The menthol box was always labelled and I looked through the pile and found no menthol. It now occurred to me that one or more of his little nitro-glycerine boxes might be among them, and if so, I should have touched it without recognising it as they were unlabelled.

I at once went through the boxes, and one was there containing nitro-glycerine and one amyl-nitrite capsule. This drug he had only carried with him shortly before his death: it was therefore probably the last box he used.

The messages given from George to his wife which I had asked for in my room the night before, and which were introduced by the spoken name, may be regarded as having some evidential value, for all the matters alluded to, though quite unknown to me, were corroborated by his wife.

But the three personal proofs used – my whistle,' 'tin box,' and 'patch,' may be regarded as evidential in a very special way.

One day, a few months before he passed over, when we were discussing various things I had asked him, 'Have you ever thought how one could more conclusively prove one's identity if acting as a communicator?' He said, 'I have considered that and the more I think of it the more difficult it seems. I have come to the conclusion that the evidence given must be applicable only to oneself: it must therefore be of a very intimate and personal character and probably trivial, and it must be known only to one person, otherwise there would be no guarantee that the medium did not know it, so I believe absolute proof could only be conveyed to one person – to others it would be second-hand evidence.' In thinking over the sitting the remembrance of this conversation made me realise that not only the items of evidence themselves but the type of subject chosen was revealing of the kind of thought and personality which was behind the words uttered through the agency of the medium.

W. F. B. What I have been trying to say is that it is necessary for me to have a certain amount of contact with the Earth: it isn't necessary for all of us, but it is to those who are preparing to help in the affairs of humanity on Earth. You are my point of contact and through you and with you I gain a certain amount of experience. You remember I told you, not only last time but the time before more particularly, that there would be extraordinary atmospheric conditions.

Well, I feel there will be still more extraordinary conditions – in fact very strange conditions indeed, and that it is all a preliminary to an extraordinary revelation. I believe that I shall be permitted to take part in that revelation.

Do you remember how I wondered sometimes about revelations? I was interested in revelations of the past – not in our times only, but the revelations of bygone times, and I think that even then I had the subconscious knowledge that I should take part in something of greater moment than anything that had happened to me in my ordinary life. I had had a feeling for years that something very wonderful might happen to me. I expected that it might happen in my Earth life. I think it kept me young – always expecting something might happen.

Now I know it is going to happen here, and I am certain that I shall help in some extraordinary demonstration of spiritual life. I feel I am waiting for that. I am learning, studying so much in my present life that seems to me to be *all preparation for the revelation.*

I heard the last four words apart from the Control altogether.

F. E. B. I can hear your own voice.
W. F. B. When I try to make you hear my voice I can't: it's when it slips out.
Florrie!
F. E. B. Did you call my name?
W. F. B. Yes. Florrie!

INTRODUCTORY NOTE

'Florrie' was heard while the Control was speaking.

F. E. B. You used to call me something else. Can you tell me something that will make it quite certain that it is really you talking to me?

He usually called me 'Flo,' and his use of the name 'Florrie' used by others suddenly made me doubt if it was W. F. B. himself speaking, hence my request for a proof that it was himself and no other.

W. F. B. Leave it to me; leave it to me; I'll try.
I want to find out more of the mechanism of disease. No, I'll qualify that – I want to find out more of the mechanism of health, but I'm sure the intestinal theory is the right one.
F. E. B. The origin of all disease?
W. F. B. Nearly all. I'm not sure if it is not the cause of all disease – except that which is communicated through heredity; and even disease communicated in that way would find a better breeding ground if there were trouble of that kind. *Florrie!*

Voice heard again.

W. F. B. Go on talking, I don't want to become self-conscious. The healthy free functioning is so important that even there we must go back to the intestinal theory. I go back to it for everything.
If at an early age the intestines were kept in a healthy condition by nature's remedy – fruit juices – there would be no disease later in life. When there are many years of wrong feeding, wrong building up of the body, there is so much to undo before we can build up afresh.
We know that the body is made over afresh periodically: it should be our business to see that the periodic renewal is done with the right materials.
To ensure that there is only one thing that can be done. It

is better to cleanse the system from all remaining traces of wrong food before beginning the right – therefore there is nothing for it in cases where it can be done but starvation, the only safe way, and during that period I would wash out the system.

If possible I would wash out the system in the ordinary way of drinking water: if possible stick to that way. The other is necessary sometimes, but, where one can, employ the natural, more normal, if more indirect method, though the other is necessary in many cases.

We must avoid atrophy, therefore employ natural means.

Then I would introduce lemon first as a cleansing factor. Then I would introduce food as well as a cleanser in the shape of oranges; then we should have cleansed the system and can begin to build up gradually on the right lines. When so many years have been on wrong lines we must have a spring cleaning.

F. E. B. Would it be good for rheumatoid arthritis?
W. F. B. Yes, but it must be persisted in.
Will's here.

'Will's here' was said very clearly in direct voice, interrupting the voice of the Control.

W. F. B. I like talking bits myself in between.
F. E. B. I want you to.
W.F.B. But I can't.
F. E. B. Yes, but later on can't we try?
W. F. B. I've tried at night when you are going to sleep.
You may hear. My whistle.

'My whistle' was said very clearly in direct voice but rather as though with effort. I could not think what it meant.

F. E. B. Did you say 'my whistle?'
W. F. B. Yes, I did. Don't you remember my own little brand of whistle?

Then it all came back to me, though I had not thought of it since he passed away. When he was very happy and content he used to make a little clear whistle in breathing. I used to say, laughing, 'You are like a pussy cat purring when you are happy, only you whistle instead.' He couldn't do it at will, it just came and I always knew he was very content when I heard it. I called it 'Your little whistle.'

> W. F. B. If I'm interested in what I'm talking about to you, a little gush of feeling comes, and then I find a little gush of words have got over the border; there is a border, and it's easier to cross it from my side than from yours.
> It's jumping down from a height which is easier than jumping up. There is a border, and though we can overcome it, it is a difficulty.
> You know I told you about a man – a friend who passed over? I want you to know he is progressing well: he's made up for much: he made good to such an extent on Earth when he could, that he hadn't very much to make up.
> F. E. B. I want to be sure whom you are speaking of. How did he die?
> W. F. B. He wasn't ill, he took his own life. *Edward.*

The name was heard distinctly apart from the Control.

> F. E. B. I heard you say that name.
> W. F. B. I enjoy trying to talk in this way, but I'm not very interested in trumpet séances.
> F. E. B. Did it make you tired?
> W. F. B. Yes, a little. If only one need not use the trumpet, but the guides told me it magnified the sound, though I thought it disguised the voice.

I had had a sitting with Mrs. Wriedt, the voice medium, recently during the few days she was in London.

W. F. B. *George.* It's someone who has passed over. There is someone belonging to him on the Earth still. He was married, his wife is on Earth.

I heard the name in direct voice. I had asked at home the day before in my own room if he could find George, the husband of a friend of mine who could not believe he still really lived. I gave the full name and some details about the wife, whom he knew.

F. E. B. Do I know her?
W. F. B. Yes. He's trying to get through to his wife to help her. George said November had been an important month in their lives and that it had been important on two occasions. There was a third occasion too, but not so personally important. Twice in November great changes had happened. You'll be seeing George's wife soon.

She came to stay with me in December.

W. F. B. Do you know anyone called Ella or Ellen connected with George? Someone on your side he sees and likes.

His cousin Ellen had been staying with his wife.

W. F. B. Do you know if George's wife was moved from one place to another? Because he has been very interested in the move and he has tried to help her in all material matters which have not been easy for her.

Quite correct. All these items were unknown to me.

W. F. B. I think George has been rather disappointed at the attitude of one or two people – his friends – he thought they would have been more helpful.
Mother's here.

INTRODUCTORY NOTE

Direct voice heard again.

F. E. B. Mine or yours?
W. F. B. Mine. She gives you her love.
F. E. B. Have you seen the clergyman's son?
W. F. B. I'm glad you reminded me of that; I had a message. The boy has greatly improved. I promised to send his love and to say he was with them on a recent birthday.
There is someone whose name begins with J – not his father – the boy wanted him to know he had been helping.
He's trying to show me he was helping his father in a rather important gathering which took place a little while ago at which his father was interested.

Very appropriate to the circumstances at the time, though unknown to me.

W. F. B. The boy likes to be with his father and asks me to say he is with him very often. He tries to make his father feel his presence, but he isn't anxious about it because he knows his father will realise that he lives.
Tin box.

Direct voice heard.

F. E. B. What is it, darling?
W. F. B. Nothing special – only I know you will remember the old tin box and how I used it.
F. E. B. Cash-box or box with papers?

I thought of a cash-box containing some letters which were destroyed and then of a large box which contained all the material on dowsing.

W. F. B. No, not the cash-box or the box with papers in it – much smaller: you've touched one of them lately.

F. E. B. Was it one you used to take away with you with your medicines in it?

I was thinking of a box with medicine tubes in it which I had taken away with me recently and had therefore touched.

W. F. B. I kept it secreted on my person.
F. E. B. What did you use it for?

(The Control pretended to open a little box, saying, 'Something round in it – he takes one out and holds it to his mouth.') Then I knew at once he was referring to a tiny tin box with nitro-glycerine tablets which he always carried in his pocket and had at his bedside. One was always in the pocket of his dress clothes. But I had not touched that box recently, and said so.

W. F. B. Never mind. I'll make you remember at the right time. Sometimes when going visiting I was almost in a panic for fear I left them behind.
F. E. B. I ought to have remembered them for you.
W. F. B. You used to ask me sometimes if I had them.
I want you – but I must wait. You can't come yet.
F. E. B. Perhaps I'm not ready yet.
W. F. B. Few of us are ever ready to go.
F. E. B. I'm sure you were.
W. F. B. I'd like to have been more ready, but I was fairly well ready.
Patch. Do you remember? Something you laughed at that I would insist on wearing; it showed.
I don't think you liked it. But you like it now because I used it. You thought I ought to get a new one.
We talked about it when we were going away in the summer – had a little discussion about it – something with a patch on it, and you said why didn't I get a new one – the summer before I passed away.

'Patch' was heard in direct voice. At first I could not think what he meant, but when he mentioned going away I remembered.

His clothes were laid out by the maid for packing and I saw a patch on a pyjama jacket, and said, 'You cannot take a patched jacket.' He said, 'Yes, I can. Nellie did it for me because I like that soft silk very much, it's nicer than any new one.' He could not be induced to let me get new ones of the same kind to take away.

W. F. B. I'm trying to arrange another sitting this week – Friday.
F. E. B. Would you like me to come alone or bring a friend?
W. F. B. Oh! Come alone. I want you to *know* – to be *sure*: the more surely you know the more you can help other people. I want to say little things like 'tin box' and I can do it better when alone. I want to make you know.

CHAPTER 8

February 11, 1928
Leonard Sitting
Mrs. W. and F. E. B. present.

How it happened that Mrs. W. was at this Sitting. Mrs. W. had been sufficiently interested to allow me to ask W. F. B. in my own home to get a message from her husband George, if it were possible. The result of this request was recorded in the sitting of September 26, 1927.

It impressed her very much, but she did not wish to come to a sitting herself.

Her husband had often expressed a strong objection to Spiritualism.

A week or two before February 11, while writing at my bureau in Town, a sudden impulse came to me like a message: 'Ask Mrs. W. to spend the weekend February 11-14 with you.' But I remembered at once that she had told me she was engaged for that weekend.

Still I felt impelled to do it and sent the invitation.

I had the reply I expected, that she was specially engaged for that weekend and could not come.

Early in February I went to a Leonard Sitting with Archdeacon and Mrs. Talbot. During the sitting, which did not concern me, I seemed to have a definite message impressed on my mind: 'Ask for a sitting next Friday.' I knew it was impossible to get a sitting at such short notice, so I discarded it. However, when the sitting was over I asked Mrs. Leonard if she could give me any earlier date than that fixed for my next sitting. She said, as I expected, that it was impossible. I then asked, somewhat absurdly, 'Could you give me next Friday?' She replied, 'Yes I believe I could, for the lady coming that day would like to change.' Later she altered the date to Saturday afternoon.

The Talbots returned with me to my cottage to tea, and while there a telephone message came from other friends of mine to say that at a sitting on January 12, W. F. B. had spoken and given three messages for me which were quite incomprehensible to them, but they gave them in case I might understand.

The messages were as follows:

(1) 'Give love to my wife. I have been helping her specially lately. She has been thinking what to do about my papers. I have been impressing her to put them in order herself.'
(2) 'I am helping George and we are going to do all we can to get through to his wife. I shall be with George. We will make the opportunity; we have been preparing "it".'
(3) 'I am attending to the others and to the Scot.'
'This is, of course, Greek to you, but my wife will understand why I am saying it.'

These messages were quite clear to me, but I did not believe that Mrs. W. could be brought to a sitting at which her husband would speak.

On returning home to London I found a letter from Mrs. W. saying the most unlikely thing had released her and she could come to the cottage February 11-14. The sister whose duties she had undertaken for that weekend had suddenly changed her mind about going on a visit to some friends.

She said frankly, 'I don't know why I don't want to go, for I enjoy it there very much, but I do not wish it now and I am definitely not going.' I had now to break it to Mrs. W. that thinking she would not be with me I had taken a sitting for Saturday afternoon, and hoped

INTRODUCTORY NOTE

she would not mind if I left her to rest after lunch while I went to the sitting.

Late Friday evening a telephone message came from Mrs. Leonard asking could the sitting be Saturday morning at eleven.

I said 'Yes' and rang off – but realised too late (Mrs. L. had no telephone) that I should not have time to drive Mrs. W. to the cottage and get back to the 11 a.m. appointment. Saturday morning, therefore, I asked her if she would come with me to Mrs. L.'s house and go for a walk while I had my sitting. We could then drive on to the cottage together in time for lunch.

She said, 'I have a book I will read in the car.' As we arrived it began to rain, and it was an open car. I said, 'Will you sit in the lounge?' She said, 'No, I have not sought this sitting in any way and have been brought to it in spite of my will. I am not going to refuse any further.' So she came in to the sitting with me. I introduced her to Mrs. Leonard as a friend on her way to spend the weekend at my cottage in the country.

That is the actual account of how it came about that Mrs. George W. was present at the sitting on February11, 1928.

> W. F. B. I have someone with me; George, because George wanted to speak to someone, not you; he is not very interested in you – another lady.
> Did George pass over rather quickly? He had been ill towards the end and then he got weak suddenly. Now he is so pleased that he is well again and able to do things he wanted to. He was not able to keep going to the end as I did. George was very tired, but he had wonderful will power and vitality that kept him up.

He died of heart failure after influenza. The end was sudden and unexpected.

> W. F. B. He is with J.S. She (i.e. Mrs. W.) ought to know him. J.S. is someone connected with him that he has met over there – a man he knew many years ago. J.S. are initials.

And on the other side W.S. too, both men he has been very interested with.

He was more connected with them when young, in his early life.

He has been trying to get in touch with that lady to help her since he passed over. He went back to her very quickly – she had a wearing, difficult time, he had to help her through. Very few realised the conditions of what she had been passing through before. They were only judging it as an ordinary occurrence. He tried to give help mentally and spiritually.

He did not know much about the other side before he passed over, but was very glad to find such a real world that he could begin again in.

He did not know it would be solid.

George has had to work hard; he felt he must do his best over there to justify himself.

He has been able to help others on that side and others on the Earth who have difficult mental conditions.

G. I help those who have difficult intellectual conditions either before or after they come over. I believe that will be my work for some time to come.

And I have sympathy now through experience of my own.

Control: Was he a little worried or anxious before he passed over?

W. F. B. He did not realise how he got there. He said, 'I ought not to be here, I ought to go back on the Earth, seeing to things and doing things.' He had to look back on a little mental blank and he could not piece things together. It worried him. 'I ought to be back facing things,' he felt. 'What a muddle – what a difficulty there will be.' He would have worried terribly if certain people had not come to tell him not to think about it. They made him realise that he had now a brain clear and efficient, a new nervous system, and in fact that he was not to look back or try to think too much. It took him a little time to

INTRODUCTORY NOTE

become accustomed to the new conditions in his new body. It was wonderful to have no depression or anxiety. Here he says there is hopefulness; one sees ahead, but one sees clearly: it makes all the difference.
He does not remember what happened for some hours before he passed over. He says, 'I was not myself, the real "I" was not conscious.'
G. I must have done certain things unconsciously. The upper mind must have been suspended.
W. F. B. He is quite happy in his present conditions. He would not like to come back to the physical world again, though he says, ' I do not think I should shirk responsibility.'
M.W. Is there anything you would like done?
G. I think you have done most of the things I wished. I have been impressing you.
M.W. Have they been done as you wanted?
G. Yes, they have been.
A place with which I used to be connected and lived in is going to be occupied by someone else.

The house in which he had lived for many years had been vacant for some time. A former student of his who was devoted to his memory had just been appointed to a post in his University, and directly he heard that his professor's house was available he would not consider any other. He took it and lived there for several years. Then the house was sold.

G. I am pleased about that. I helped to arrange it. I tried to bring it about lately, but I began working on it before it happened.
W. F. B. Things look as though they were going to settle better now – material and financial things – it will work out all right. He was rather worried when he first passed over whether some money would be transferred or not. Not a pound or two; a good sum. He was afraid it would be difficult. On the whole things have turned out better than he expected.

He says 'it is the law of compensation working.' George was a very kind man.

He had much sympathy and bigness of heart.

If there were any people like children or poor people who wanted help he was always ready to give it. He had a brilliant brain. But though he is so clever he always kept a childlikeness. He liked simple things. He lived close to nature, close to the sincere.

He was always natural and intensely sincere.

An elderly lady is with him – medium height, grey hair parted in the middle. She has a nice-shaped face, oval, with well-cut features. She is dressed rather old-fashioned looking. She passed over before him.
M.W. This well describes his mother.
W. F. B. And a younger lady also looked after him.
There is an elderly gentleman with him too – taller than me, heavier built; he is grey and has rather a clever face and head; he has a Roman nose. He has a rather distinguished face – a dignified looking gentleman. He was in the spirit world before George and had been trying to help him on Earth. He was one of the first to meet him when he passed over. When George saw him, at once he felt comforted. The gentleman put out both hands and held his. George knew he'd be safe with him; the grip of that man's hands helped him. He was a man for whom he'd had great respect and often talked about him. He had a portrait of him in his house, a good one: he was very pleased to meet him.
M.W. G.W. on leaving College was secretary for several years to an elderly and distinguished politician, and a life-long friendship was formed. No other man ever took his place or influenced him so much. He had been dead for six or seven years. His portrait – a reproduction of a painting – was the only one that ever hung in our house.

INTRODUCTORY NOTE

W. F. B. Annie – he keeps saying Annie – there is a lady – passed over many years ago.
M.W. Annie, his only sister, died in 1917.
W. F. B. Kate – a lot of people gather round him. I think he was an easy person to get on with. He was welcome wherever he went. He has quite a lot of little gatherings; he shines in them – lives in a whirl of them. When I go to see him he has quite a little congregation round him all talking. He is very popular here.
M.W. A very true picture. His students and others – all kinds of people – were constantly coming to consult him. Intellectual difficulties, private troubles, economic hindrances, all found ready sympathy and understanding and often financial help.
W. F. B. There is another gentleman – late middle age. He knew him very well here and was related to him. A man he was pleased to see. C. You will know later.
It is not Charles, though he's seen Charles – but a friend he used to know years ago. (? two syllables.)
M.W. Carrington
W. F. B. Whom did he know who was fond of fishing? George used to get a bit bored by fishing.
M.W. His brother Charles was fond of fishing.
W. F. B. He has met such a lot of old friends.
F. E. B. How did you come to meet him?
W. F. B. Well – I just linked up with him. You wanted me to, and asked me to help him. Did you know I tried to bring George to the other sitting but couldn't push him through properly?

This 'asking' was never done at a sitting, but in my own room at home. At a recent sitting with another medium he got through the name 'George,' but that was all.

W. F. B. Have you been thinking of one or two things to do before you come over? The difficult problem is my papers – psychical and other papers. You cannot deal with all those – cannot do anything until you are clear of your own things.

Shelve them for the time being till you know more what you are doing for the next year or two.

He had arranged his papers into those relating to psychic matters and scientific papers. I had been thinking how it would be possible to find time to go into the question as to whether any of these should be published.

W. F. B. Another friend of mine is coming to talk about the old days. I know you can't always be seeing people I used to know. You do when you can, but you have other things to do with people not connected with them.

Philip Somerville-Large came soon after to stay a few days with me. He is a very old friend of W. F. B. I had been seeing two or three of his old friends.

F. E. B. Have you sent messages by St. Bruno?
W.F.B. I understand – yes, I did.
Control: He smiled as he answered.

This friend had given me messages, one of which said: 'George and I are determined to get through to one on the Earth and I am arranging it.' The recognition of the name St. Bruno was evidence of memory of Earth times, for it had never been used by anyone at a Leonard Sitting before.

W. F. B. I have been so pleased to meet the astronomer.

Flammarion, the French astronomer, whose friendship gave him much pleasure on Earth.

W. F. B. We get together and look through telescopes. Oh! we do have some interesting hours together, *absorbingly* interesting. I haven't been to visit other planets, but we are cognisant of the life there.

F. E. B. Are they inhabited?
W. F. B. They are inhabited, but a different form of life, yet belonging to the same system. Those in the same solar system must necessarily conform to the same type. They differ in stature and shape to a certain extent.
F. E. B. Have they intelligence?
W. F. B. Undoubtedly. A planet with physical and no mental life would be dead to us. Life which lives by instinct is like lower plant life.

The life of reason is shared with higher animals – life higher than human is spirit rather than intelligence. We share spirit with higher beings as animals share intellect with us.

As we help to raise animals, so angels help to raise us even on Earth to reach the fringes of the spiritual.

F. E. B. Can you get further than we?
W. F. B. Yes, it is easier for us to grasp the teaching of spiritual beings, and go ahead with them. We're not confused and limited by the appeal to the physical senses. On Earth it's right there should be an appeal to the physical so as to live; directly it stops you pass over, or are in an unconscious condition.

When a limb is no longer sensitive to touch, something has happened to paralyse it, to deaden it – so we must use our senses and allow them to be appealed to. But the trouble is, do we allow them to be appealed to in a constructive or in a destructive way? If we allow our senses to be appealed to in such a way that they distract and confuse us and take our attention from things of the spirit world, then it is wrong.

The things that appeal too much, e.g. drink, greed, anything that leads to selfishness, are bad; yet the same senses may respond to physical things that suggest pity, sympathy, understanding, and if we bring these things into the revealing light of spiritual truth we are doing that for which we were sent on Earth.

We are each of us sent on Earth to reveal truth, which means really revealing God. We can reveal truth in the smallest action, in the simplest word, and we should strive to do so every moment of the day. But those who become slaves to the

senses instead of master are living on the lower plane of being to which the lower animals and the vegetable kingdom belong. That is why I say you must live above the senses, not immersed in them, and always using them wisely and with understanding and discretion, not suppressing or ignoring them but using them. The same sense and the same force which means exhibition of energy which can lead a man to kill someone or strike a blow in anger can be used and diverted into a channel for good. Therefore one must not suppress energy but transmute it—making a bad condition into a good one.
Don't we often waste time on bad conditions instead of trying to superimpose a good condition?
The law is that good shall conquer whether in sin or in matters of health. Good must conquer if it gets a chance.
I am interested in healing and I am going to help you a good deal in that way. I can do it more later on because opportunities to put into practice will come.
It would be rather difficult at the moment for you to put into practice all I could tell you to do. People would think you had gone mad.
We're all potential channels for healing. You're a channel for the healing power. When I was on Earth I know your magnetism and healing power was helpful to me and kept me up. I'm quite sure of it, and I always remember; I know you have healing power apart from the knowledge of medicine and surgery. Later on there will be opportunities for trying to use it.
A. is here. She is wanting to send her love to the other lady.

I.e. to M.W., who was a great friend of hers from girlhood.

W. F. B. She is so happy and busy; she has the home of her dreams. I think you would call A. a spiritual mother. Hands out to all who need.
George sends all his love to his wife.
M. W. Does he know I am going away?
W. F. B. He knows and approves.

CHAPTER 9

August 11, 1928
Leonard Sitting

W. F. B. There are several things I want to write through you with regard to healing and the functions of the soul independently of, and also in relation to, the body.

I am particularly anxious to explain in simple language the possibilities of developing conscious or objective manifestations from the soul body, which we call the etheric body, the body which is around you and in you now, which is part of the physical but independent of it.

I feel that all spiritual inspiration, communication, and also all treatment that affects the physical body comes through and affects the etheric body first.

What you call subconsciousness resides in – locates itself in – the brain of the etheric body; the consciousness of objective sense resides in the physical brain; now what we want to aim at is a better co-operation between the two. If we have co-operation between the two we have perfect sanity, perfect health, greater measure of happiness and wisdom because through the association with the etheric body one reaches out to the source of inspiration and life.

How I hope that through you I can make people understand the importance of recognising and cooperating with the etheric body and brain: mind is the power that acts on the brain. The etheric brain is a mechanism, a channel on which the mind operates just as the physical brain is.

In the spirit world (I don't like the word but it saves trouble if I use it – I can't keep saying 'in this world where people have escaped from the flesh') there are lower planes than that on which I exist.

Those lower planes are unhappy, sad, depressing places; they are peopled with souls who have had no, or very little consciousness of the spiritual self during the soul's residence in the physical body, and who, therefore, have no conscious life, no independent life in the creative mental self.

What I want to do, and my great aim now, is to show people on Earth the importance of developing the soul or etheric life *before* they leave the body, so that they can avoid residence in these lower planes. I hope to do that later through you – with you. We are all trying to help you to teach others the imperative urgency of living the spiritual life whilst still in the physical. The spiritual life must be formed in the physical life: that is the object for which God created the Earth and the physical life thereon.

I knew so much more relating to this subject than the average individual when I was here, therefore I was better equipped for understanding more regarding it after passing over.

The whole point to my mind is:

(*1*) The recognition that there is a soul and therefore some body as a vehicle.//
(2) If there is a vehicle, the consciousness of it, co-operation with it, and above all knowledge of it.

F. E. B. Why explain knowledge of it?//
W. F. B. Because, my dear, through knowledge of it will come the ability to draw the power of the spirit through it.

INTRODUCTORY NOTE

You see your car; you know it's there; surely the more you *understand* your car the more you can get out of it.

You have a bottle of medicine. If you just say, 'That is a bottle of medicine; I'll take it anyhow, any time, because it's there,' you can't expect the same results as if you understood what it is, what it is for and how to use it.

What we want to do is to give people, or help them to give themselves, this power which is largely unused and wasted in the background of their physical lives.

There are two results to be gained from the recognition and the knowledge:

(*1*) The advantage it gives in the Earth life.
(*2*) The advantage it gives after passing over.

Many people will ask, 'What advantage does it give in the Earth life? I can see what advantage it may have in the afterlife.' It opens the gates of inspiration; the intuition is keener, and with that comes greater enthusiasm, greater understanding of the beauties in life, even the perceiving of beauty where formerly ugliness appeared to exist. There is power, a help that comes through co-operation with the etheric body that will also certainly help the physical well-being and health. We speak often of the recuperative powers and the natural resistance of nature. We know nature is fighting disease, struggling to overcome every ill flesh is heir to. We can increase that power of resistance because the etheric body has no disease, is impervious to disease; yet it is a body, and if we are aware of that body, in touch with it, we can draw upon the life, or the magnetic currents of that body in order to recharge the life currents, the life essence in the physical. You know, dear, I often come with you, I often use you as a pair of spectacles with which to perceive and check certain conditions on Earth. I have noticed that in all unhealthy or diseased persons the magnetic current or amount of magnetic power in the body is decreased – below average. I think it was a stumbling after this truth that caused us to discover and use electricity, *but* we cannot supply the same kind of electricity as that electro-magnetic flow which should be drawn from the etheric body.

That is why we see many cases that fail to respond to electrical treatment. I feel we can help humanity a very great deal by:

(*1*) Showing them there is this other body.
(2) How to get in touch with it.
(3) What it will mean if they do.

I like the flowers you brought. They're for *me*, not for her. I wanted you to bring them and then the Medium can have them after the sitting.

Sometimes I used to point out flowers and leaves to you. I knew a good deal about them; for example, I used to say, 'That is so and so, or it belongs to such and such a family.' I knew more than you did, so I used to explain them to you. I'm saying that not only because you've brought some flowers today, but because you were puzzling about the name and origin of a plant lately, a tall one, Acanthus.

A few days before, when looking over the plants in the herbaceous border, I could not think of the name of one and wished he were there to tell me, as he always knew, or if he didn't know would look it up.

The day after I lunched with a friend who was an expert gardener herself. I was early and she asked me to walk down the garden. There was the plant which I had not been able to name, and I said, 'What is its name? I cannot remember, though I know it well.' She replied, 'It's odd you should ask me that, for when I woke this morning something suggested to me you would ask the name of the plant suggestive of architecture.'

W. F. B. I love being with you among the plants and I think it's good for you. I sometimes begrudge the time when you can't be with them.

INTRODUCTORY NOTE

> I don't advocate you ever submerging yourself in rural life, but I do like you to have more time there. At present I don't see how you can, but a little later on I think you will be able to, so it's worthwhile holding on with that prospect in view.
> F. E. B. Have you heard anything of the child I spoke of?

The day before at home I had asked if he could find the child of a friend who had died recently. The only clue to her I could give was that her mother lunched with us the day that W. F. B. died.

> W. F. B. I have been interested in a child, *not* on Earth, one who passed over. This is a child passed over rather lately and I have taken care of it at its passing – I received the child. There was some link in a roundabout way.
> B. is someone connected with the child, who was in the child's unconscious mentality on waking.
> Why did she feel so chokey? Something made it feel difficult in breathing: this was an impression brought over with her – not now.
> She didn't suffer much – wouldn't suffer in passing at all.
> F. E. B. What was her name?
> W. F. B. V is the letter I want. Vi.
> There is a lady on Earth I want you to help about her. The lady's very sad because of this. The child gives me the name Nanny too, and a name beginning with M. Not M for mother, but a name. There is another girl on Earth connected with her too.
> The child Vi is all right and she is going to be very happy when she understands a little more. She is not *unhappy*.
> Seven is a number connected with her.

Spoken very clearly.

> She is learning, developing and being taken care of. There are many things she'll enjoy and appreciate. She will never be ill, always in perfect health.

I think she might not have been so if she had lived, so it will be happier for her.

Before she passed over there was something the matter with one arm or hand; she couldn't move it.

At the end did she pass quickly – just at the end – rather a shock her passing. She was ill, but the end came rather quickly – she seemed better, then was ill again.

A. has taken a great interest in her too. Vi has other people, relatives nearer to her, but I thought you would like me to keep an eye on her. She has already taken a proprietary interest in me and I can't help being fond of her, for she has a very sweet disposition. She's showing *a great spirit of curiosity* – 'What does this mean?' 'What is all this?' 'Why is it there?' are her questions.

She has a very intelligent mind, a very quick brain, a natural understanding, not one that comes from just learning things: she loves colour and flowers.

What birthday was she thinking of when she passed over? – she spoke of 'birthday.' I think they'll understand. She's been taken to see her people: she will be a good deal with them a little later. Will you remember to give her love to them because she does love them so much, and they her – there is such a strong bond between them.

I do help people sometimes with whom there is not the same strong bond of love, and then it is very difficult, but there is a strong bond with Vi.

My friend was in great distress through the loss of her little girl, who had died after a short illness.

I had no knowledge of the nature of the illness, but on August 10 I had asked W. F. B. if he could find the child and get any message or evidence that might comfort her mother. The following facts were given to me by her mother after the sitting.

The child was seven years old. Her illness was measles followed by pneumonia and encephalitis, hence the difficulty in breathing and the paralysis of one arm and leg.

INTRODUCTORY NOTE

She was nursed by her mother and Nanny. M is the initial of her favourite school teacher of whom she spoke in her illness. Ben was a great friend whose letter telling about his birthday was read to her shortly before she became unconscious.

She had one sister. Her name was Violet, but Vi was the name used in her family.

> W. F. B. I find it very easy to be a bridge. Perhaps I am more successful than most in obtaining messages: you and I have helped several: it comes easy to me.
> I can probably give their messages for them even better than themselves. Perhaps it is because I was well grounded in the subject and its difficulties.
> I feel that you and I have a great deal to do together in helping people to understand there is this afterlife.

CHAPTER 10

March 9, 1929
Barkel Sitting

In a sitting with Mrs. Barkel on March 9, 1929, some messages were of interest because of the connection with messages through other sources.
Mrs. Barkel's control is an Indian called Whitehawk.

Whitehawk: (Control) Do you come here to keep an appointment with a gentleman? He tells me he has an appointment with you.
I have seen him before, this gentleman, bringing a little girl.

Vi's mother had gone for a sitting anonymously to Mrs. Barkel.

He says: 'You told me to; you asked me to help about it. I hope I did it to your satisfaction.'
Were you not pleased that he was able to help and comfort? Anything he could do he said he would.
He is giving me a date 1884 to 1885. Something outstanding to him – something he started.
He says he finds he has to give separate little bits through this medium.
He is showing me a book again, on the back is S.P.R. 18-92.

The medium acts as though turning over pages.

He says page 92 or the opposite, 29. On that page 95 there is some reference to himself which will interest you; he thinks it characteristic and evidential.

I looked at the Proceedings and Journals of the S.P.R. for 1892 on pages 29 and 92, but found nothing to confirm. It then occurred to me that the turning over leaves might have been done to show Whitehawk 92 referred to pages not dates when he said 92, so using 1884 as date I found it was the first number of the S.P.R. Journal and the book opened at an introductory letter from W.F.B., which seems to suggest that it was he who proposed the Journal and was appointed first editor. Of this I had no previous knowledge.

Opening the book at page 92, I find opposite the following note: 'Professor Barrett made some remarks in which he reminded those present of the distinction between genuine thought-transference where the idea is impressed without contact or movement, and the "muscle reading" of public exhibitions.'

Whitehawk: Little Violet says may she send love to her Mummy and her Daddy and he sends his love.

The name Violet was spontaneously given.

Whitehawk: Do you remember a rough-haired dog? It is in connection with another house than that you are living in now, with grass and larger spaces. He has him with him.

See previous reference to this dog in a Leonard Sitting on April 9, 1926. It was a Griffon who was his constant companion when we lived at Longcross House, which had wide lawns and open spaces – the only small dog belonging to me which had died.

F. E. B. Have you spoken to me elsewhere lately?
Yes, but not very long: there was not a great deal of power.

INTRODUCTORY NOTE

> I was there and the power in itself was very good, but why didn't it last longer? Did you get the message about the book?
> F. E. B. Yes.
> W. F. B. I meant it as a test – a kind of book test very much on the lines we were interested in. It was not only good, it was characteristic. You got the book right, but you got the wrong book first. They mixed the page with the book, but you got the right one after; the numbers were transposed.
> Now I will give you another little test from the same book. I want you to look at the third page; it is a corroboration of the previous message: not the third page of the book but the third page of the first long reading matter – a curious similarity with what I gave before.

On the third page of the 'first long reading matter,' i.e. page 5 of the book, are two references of special interest to W.F.B.

'A note on the Sensory Effects of Magnetism was read by Professor Barrett. The author stated that the result of recent experiments which he had made pointed in the direction of a peculiar sensation being produced by a powerful magnet upon certain organisations. As this was opposed to the general opinion of scientific men, and the experience of those who are in the habit of working daily with large magnets, more evidence is required.'

The next paper on 'The Divining Rod,' prepared by Mr. S. R. Pease, was read. Dowsing was a subject to which W. F. B. had given special attention and had published reports of his work.

> W. F. B. Apart from this Medium it was the best sitting I've had – only the power didn't last. I was afraid of dragging it out because that's where mistakes occur. *It was an Indian Control.*

This was in the direct voice.

> Control: He says an Eastern was in command.
> F. E. B. I heard your voice say 'It was an Indian Control.'

85

W. F. B. You hear my voice, the Medium gets my thoughts. *Indian is correct.*

Direct voice again.

F. E. B. Have you spoken with me at home?
W. F. B. Yes, by spelling. It was rather laborious but very interesting. Twice I tried to spell out LOVE and it was nipped in the bud each time.

We had tried table turning at home with scattered messages.

You put a lot into me – your wonderful vitality and magnetism. You might say it was care and thought, but you kept me going till I had to go over.
What it meant to me I cannot tell you till you come. I hated the thought of being incapacitated: I disliked the thought intensely, and you kept me going – in those ways you used your power: it was transmutation of power. Many people have psychic power and use it in their various professions – musicians, artists, etc. If not they would probably develop as mediums.
I believe we have many things to do together before you pass over. I feel there is work for us to do – something definite to do together, and I shall be allowed to come much closer for that purpose.
It wasn't chance we came together on Earth.
Looking back, did you or I realise what it would lead to? I had no idea it would lead to such understanding and happiness and affection, and I know it and recognise it more even since I passed over than I did before. *It was intended.*

Direct voice.

It happened in a strange way, led up to by a series of steps, and neither of us understood the importance or depth of it at the time. We were both drawn into it by others who were guiding us in the right direction. I did not understand at the time all it might mean, and we know others didn't understand. Very few who belong to us understand what you and I mean to each other, because they only look at the surface: they could not see deeply. You know it more now, don't you? How important it was that you and I should belong to each other. Now you are carrying on my work as well as your own. You made me very happy and comfortable here, but happier still now.

It doesn't matter about other people: when we all meet on this side, as we inevitably shall, it will all be right, all clear, all understood.

I want you to know I shall always understand anything you do: I shall always know whatever it is you do, it's for the best.

CHAPTER 11

～

May 25, 1929
Leonard Sitting

W. F. B. I feel we must simplify life. There are important matters you must seek to keep yourself free for, things that others can't do but you can.
I am working with you now in so many ways.
I shall shortly be able to impress you more and more strongly than ever before.
My mission in life is to work with you; we were brought together for that purpose. I used to think that you were brought to me to help in many ways on Earth. It was not so; we were brought together for a definite purpose in accordance with plans made for us on this side. They were good plans which will result in our spiritual advancement and have already done so.
Were you wondering what to do about some books of mine? I was even more puzzled than you would be what to do with them. They are not worth your keeping. I thought they might be made use of in some institution. They are not stories but scientific books, books of travel too. You may think of what to do and whatever you do I shall be pleased.
I have no particular wish about any material things I

possessed; I leave decisions about them to you and I know it will be all right.

F. E. B. Tell me something about your own doings.

W. F. B. You know I am happy, don't you? I tried to tell you that. I have a life of useful activity, so busy and so interesting. By the way, why were you thinking of my passing over again? It was only the passing into a fuller life for me, so I always ask you to rejoice over it.

Since I passed over I found out that so much prayer is almost useless because it is done in a too formal way. Prayer should be made as simple as possible. A natural thought sent out to God is much better than a stereotyped and set prayer performed at a stated time and therefore often given mechanically. We often forget what prayer is. It is talking to our Father – that is what prayer should be – asking for our Father's guidance and help. Much of so-called prayer is a request for gifts, for material advantages. That is wrong. But we may ask for enlightenment to prepare ourselves for good in our physical lives. I feel we may ask for that; we have been told we may ask for our daily bread which embraces all possible need, but we are not told to ask for tomorrow's daily bread. I feel the words 'Give us this day our daily bread' mean that we have to be satisfied with each day's supplies, and we shall be given them if we ask simply and directly for them.

I think you sometimes find yourself in a little difficulty in regard to prayer. Do not feel apologetic towards God if at times you cannot feel the sense of God and spiritual communion as you would wish to. You can talk to God at any time, in the car, in the street, in a restaurant and in the country. God is everywhere. He does not wish you to make great effort in order to provide what you may think a fitting place in which to speak to Him.

Prayer is most powerful; it is almost our only way of opening ourselves to strength and wisdom.

I know of no better way, and I am sure it would not matter what the trouble was, there would be some alleviation of it if you would open yourself to the source of strength and to the help that is never denied.

We pray over here, but we pray naturally.

F. E. B. Do you pray without vision?

W. F. B. Yes, and no. It depends on what I am doing. Sometimes I find myself doing something for which I want help. I simply speak and ask for that help.

But at other times I find I attain a remarkable degree of clairvoyance. As I lift my soul up in prayer true vision comes to me. I feel God, I understand God. I see all kinds of wonderful visions which in themselves lift and stimulate me. But often on the Earth you have to pray blindly and as you say without vision, but sometimes that blind stumbling on the threshold of the spiritual world opens the gate and the vision comes when we least expect it. We may think we are praying without vision, but the very act of prayer will or should bring vision with it. I have seen many men begin to pray hopelessly, but they have prayed feeling 'Is this thing any use? I cannot see anything or feel anything'; and yet the words of prayer rise from their lips, and though while they are praying they may feel nothing, afterwards peace comes, and after peace strength and inspiration. I have seen that again and again.

Do not be afraid of worrying God; talk to Him all day if you want to. What father would complain of his children wanting to speak to him? Go on talking and vision will come, more strength and more vision.

November 5, 1929
LEONARD SITTING

W. F. B. I have been to another Medium to send a kind of message through to you. I thought I was clever to push myself through and get it to you by proxy.

Miss Bazett met me by chance later and said, 'Sir William came to me one day but only said I was to give you his love and to be sure and use the names Flo or Florence, not the intermediate one with two syllables.'

W. F. B. *Florrie*. I shall always take the opportunity of doing this *if I can*.

Direct voice.

W. F. B. The time is coming for you to give out the results of our communication.
F. E. B. Shall I know when?
W. F. B. I will impress you, and guide you over every detail. We have a mass of evidence of a peculiar type, but there are other things behind the evidence which I want to bring out. On my side I see and feel what should be the guiding principles of life clearly, with absolute clarity of vision. On our side there is no justification for the slogan that you can do evil that good may come– you cannot – even if good appears to come it is but a dangerous semblance of a beneficial condition. That which is founded on good *and* is *good in itself* is productive of lasting good. Some of these things from time to time I shall tell you. I will corroborate as much as I possibly can. I mean, *Florrie* (heard), that I will corroborate in as many different conditions as possible so that you will feel you are on firm ground.
I was extremely interested and touched on my arrival into spiritual life by finding that I was held to have been a pioneer, a worker for the spiritual world. What a strange thing that you have to be a pioneer too! At one time you yourself would have thought it an almost impossible condition, but it is your work as I now find it was mine *and is still*. Do not hurry about this matter; I will tell you when to begin.

Much direct voice.

INTRODUCTORY NOTE

> My object in coming to you and helping you, apart from the personal object, is to point out a definite, simple and easy way to the puzzled people on Earth.
> I do not only want to add to the mass of evidence already given. I want to have additional evidence given, but I want to point the way as well. Life on my side seems so extraordinarily easy compared to Earth, because we simply live according to the rules of love.

Here came an effort to give evidence from a Col. R., husband of a friend of mine, but could not recollect a name he had given.

> When I am in my own sphere I am told a name and think I shall remember it; when I come into the conditions of a sitting I then know that I can only carry with me – contain in me – a small portion of my consciousness. The easiest things to lay hold of are what we may call ideas; a detached word, a proper name, has no link with a train of thought except in a detached sense; that is far more difficult than any other feat of memory or association of ideas.
> If you go to a medium that is new to us, I can make myself known by giving you through that medium an impression of my character and personality, my work on Earth and so forth. Those can all be suggested by thought, impressions, ideas; but if I want to say 'I am Will,' I find that is much more difficult than giving you a long, comprehensive study of my personality. 'I am Will' sounds so simple, but you understand that in this case the word 'Will' becomes a detached word. If I wanted to express an idea of my scientific interests I could do it in twenty different ways. I should probably begin by showing books, then giving impressions of the nature of the book and so on, till I had built up a character impression of myself, but 'I am Will' presents difficulties. I have given you the name William at another sitting.

This was true. At a sitting with a voice medium he had given the name William.

F. E. B. Why do you call me 'Florrie' at a sitting when you never used to call me so?
W. F. B. I have found it an easy name to get through at a sitting, and having once done it, it is easy to get through again; even through other mediums I shall probably get that word through.
Some time previous to your bringing his father here I had been helping Michael, but on several occasions I had brought the boy here when a sitting was being held by the S.P.R. There were three occasions.
The sitters were strangers to us. I think two were women, but I am not sure of the third. We brought Michael and gave his Christian name and part of his surname and several facts about his identity. On two occasions I was described as being with him. Full notes were taken by the official note taker of the Society. His surname was probably not quite correctly given, but a near resemblance to it. A clear description of him, however, was given, yet no one seems to remember the circumstances or to look into it. I think they were new sitters, unknown to Michael or to me. I do not like anything evidential to be passed over.
Radium. I am not quite sure yet of its efficiency.
I understand the natural healing power of light: all plant life is dependent on light.
The human body was intended to be subjected to light – the healing rays of the sun – but so-called civilisation has thwarted this; I feel it is most important to employ light rays in the building up of the vital forces. The important part is gradually to build up a new skin which will enable the blood to take up the healing power in the rays of the sun and distribute to other parts of the organism.
It is most important about radium. The sub- or semi-substance called radium must contain some extraordinarily potent factor,

INTRODUCTORY NOTE

but at the present moment I am afraid it might prove itself to be a destructive as well as a constructive, element. Radium is an eliminator; it eliminates certain factors which make for disease, but in the process shall I say, it delocalises the diseased condition, shifts it as it were. The danger is, and I want you to take note of this, that in changing the locality *very slightly* [direct voice] of the diseased condition it may transfer it to a spot where it may be extremely dangerous even if only resting there temporarily during the period of dissemination. I think events will prove the truth of my hypothesis.

F. E. B. Will radium be given up?

W. F. B. No, I cannot say it will be given up, but I think its field of utility will be changed – located first, and changed, because of this peculiar dislodging process which takes place. In the destroying of disease which undoubtedly takes place under the action of radium there is a danger; that is the reason I cannot whole-heartedly support the use of radium as yet.

CHAPTER 12

January 11, 1930
Barkel Sitting

Mrs. Barkel's Control:

Good afternoon, lady. Mr. William told me you were coming to talk to me because he was helping last night. Do they call you Flo – or Florence? Since coming over here he has carried on already his investigations along more advanced lines of thought, but it would be difficult to get some colleagues on your side to accept his theories. But they are no longer theories with him; he is observing three more planets soon to be discovered in the orbit of the sun – in this planetary system: he has mentioned it vaguely before. Owing to the erratic movements of Uranus – that is causing tempest and storm on your Earth – it has an extraordinary reverse motion on the planet.

A planet near the sun which appears and disappears will be discovered by a man of the stars on your side: then you can let it be known that he had already found it. It will probably be two or three years before there will be clear visibility.

Extract from The *Times*,
Saturday, March 15, 1930:

THE NEW PLANET

The report from Lowell University of the discovery of a new planet was received with interest by astronomers in this country yesterday, and though confirmation cannot be obtained yet either from old photographs or by new observations at English observatories, there is a general tendency to accept the news as authentic, since it agrees with predictions already made and based on the disturbance of the planet Uranus, and in a lesser degree that of Neptune.

Observation is more difficult because the planet is reported to be in a very thick part of the Milky Way. Sir Frank Dyson, the Astronomer Royal, said yesterday that its existence has been suspected for some time, having been deduced chiefly from the movements of Uranus. This matter and the predictions based on it were discussed at a meeting of the Royal Astronomical Society last night. Information had been received from the Lowell Observatory that the planet was observed for seven weeks before the announcement was made. Its position was given, and a telegram of congratulation was sent in reply.

Another paper says:

NEW PLANET
Bigger than the Earth.
Discovery in U.S.A.
Greatest since Neptune.

A new planet of the solar system, larger than the Earth, but smaller than Uranus, has been discovered at Lowell Observatory, Arizona.

INTRODUCTORY NOTE

The planet, which is beyond Neptune, makes the ninth major planet of the solar family, and its discovery is described here as the greatest event in astronomy since the discovery of Neptune 84 years ago. 'Astronomers are greatly excited at the news, which confirms the hypothesis of the late Professor Percival Lowell, who was well known in England for his Martian theories, that a ninth planet existed farther out in space than Neptune.'

Whitehawk: He says, 'What has interested me and will interest you is that the drawing near of the new planet releases unusual rays and with the sun rays will bring about a new chemical substance – gases that will blend and be beneficial in health-giving rays on Earth.' He is showing me things of light and sound. Do you remember he felt sure there must be life on the planets? Well, he has proved it in several ways.
F. E. B. How?
Whitehawk: By visiting them. On some there is more advanced humanity: on others a less advanced stage than ours. (In the moon are giant flora and fauna which seem to resemble somewhat the early ages of the Earth: in many respects it is like a deserted city.) He has found Martian humanity closest akin to earthly. He discovered there a greater knowledge of the force you call electricity. It is used for all purposes of healing. You will have heard that people have spoken of a cloud-like formation round Mars. It is surrounded by cloud which appears pinkish and golden to them, not blue and green like your cloud. Also Mars has two suns, and consequently there is less change of climate; it is clear and warm.

Here follow allusions to subjects mentioned in other Leonard Sittings or show knowledge of things in use at home, ending with messages from George to his wife and Violet to her mother. Lastly –

Anna is someone who serves you. She tells me she has come to serve you and send love from the world of spirit. She is medium height and build, with browny dark hair – plain.

She is fair, round and fresh looking. Eyes blue-grey, homely looking. Did she have pains in her chest?

This is an accurate description of a maid we called Julia: the description exactly fitted Julia, but the name was wrong. On returning home I asked a senior maid if Julia had another name, Anna. She said, 'We used to tease her by calling her Anna because her name was really Juliana.' She died in 1929 of sarcoma of the chest.

February 6, 1930
Leonard Sitting

> W. F. B. Since you came here to speak to me I have been told by those qualified to tell and teach me that it was necessary for me to meet and live in close association with someone who had your knowledge of your special subject in order that it should form a groundwork for the even more important task which you and I have to tackle together.
> I know you've often been puzzled by certain aspects of what we must call health and disease, life and death: this mysterious strength which we call the life force, which while it animates matter produces what we call on Earth health and life, and when it is withdrawn from even a small area of an individual body it leaves that area at the mercy of what we call disease – mortification. Because disease is only a stage of mortification as we see it from our side.
> If we can only induce this live force to inhabit or animate every portion of the body equally or in correct proportion we should have no disease of any kind. Old age would be simply a quiet preparation for the new country, a gentle relinquishing of the physical things in order to grasp more tangible lasting spiritual things which are awaiting one – that is what old age should be. Even in these last two months I have been investigating the etheric body, that body which is the intermediate vehicle for this mysterious force.

INTRODUCTORY NOTE

The physical body is not acted upon directly, but always through the mediumship of the etheric body.

The etheric body is the missing link and all forms of life on Earth have their etheric body.

Scientists have been puzzled as to the kind of link, if any, which exists between the animating force called life or energy, and that which we call matter.

There has been something missing in between, and this etheric counterpart or body is the missing link.

Life and energy can only work through the etheric body in order to reach and animate matter. Now I feel you and I are going to find a way of definitely attacking disease through the mediumship of this etheric body which is invisible yet tangible.

Must we deny its existence, as I know many intellectual people do, because it is invisible to our earthly eyes? The wind is invisible to our earthly eyes, but we do not deny its importance and existence.

We only recognise the wind by its manifestations.

Do we not recognise God by His manifestations? And here we are faced by another invisible but potent and all-important condition which is vitally necessary to the health and very existence of man on Earth.

What I am beginning to find out is the best way of treating the physical body so that the etheric body can become more part of it.

I have noticed in disease of any kind there is absence or partial withdrawal of the etheric counterpart of the diseased area, and I know a cure can only be effected by doing something which will induce or enable the etheric part to interpenetrate the so- called physical or material part again.

This is my work, what I am going to concentrate on in addition to my usual round of work and study.

I will report to you from time to time.

* * * * * *

> W. F. B. I am not talking about someone on Earth, but someone who passed over since you were here – you were sorry for her and wondered how she would get on.
> It was very sudden and she was in a confused mental state. She was trying to do something with her head – not suffocating – gas. Poor woman! A splendid woman. Ada and I are helping. I drew Ada into it because of her understanding.

This with later messages clearly describes a friend of mine who had spent her life in mission work and who had gassed herself while working in the East End.

> W. F. B. It was nothing more or less than overstrain. She was kind to others, conscientious, and meant well in every way. She has not been punished in any way whatever because it was no more her fault than if she had accidentally fallen and injured her brain. I told her I would tell you about it this morning, and she thanks you with loving gratitude for your thoughts of her, because she knew several people, whom she had helped and been a friend to, were picking out what they thought were her weak points and not realising that so much of her physical power and strength had been spent in the service of others.
> She was a very nice woman. I don't think you have any idea of the extent to which your thoughts helped her. We are extra-sensitive to the thoughts of those on Earth, specially in the early days when our own minds hover between the Earth we have left and the new land on which our feet are not yet firmly planted. In that between condition we need your thoughts, but we need right thoughts, constructive, helpful, loving thoughts. I shall tell her when I go back what I've told you and what you said. You know her life was becoming rather a muddle. She was tired out and could not see straight any longer. Her focussing power had temporarily gone – not her reason.

INTRODUCTORY NOTE

May 13, 1930
Leonard Sitting

> W. F. B. I often try to send little messages through other people to let you know I do not miss any *opportunity* of writing a note to you, because if I had gone to another country and could not see you I should want to write to send messages, but I should have to wait for the mail boats; so I consider these other people are mail boats and when one arrives I make use of it.
> I've been helping you a great deal lately; there will be things to settle about the country, and I shall have to help you a good deal in that way, because out of the things happening now and the next few months, there will be other things happening, more important later. The things happening now are not so all-important in themselves, but I feel more important things will happen from them – a definite outcome.
> There is a new place in the country. I like it and think it is a good thing. I am speaking of the new house. It's not finished yet, there are things to be done, I won't say unfortunately, because I shall enjoy doing them and having things as we want them. I like the *trees* – *love* them – very delightful.
> I should have liked it when I was here. You've got what I should like in this place. I like the conditions and surroundings, it's quiet, yet still within reach of *civilisation*. It's not ungetatable – wonderful for what it is.

I had just bought a cottage in the country, having sold the previous one nine months before.

> W. F. B. What about the wall – something is going to come through it, I've got a feeling of it.
> F. E. B. Do you mean a door to the balcony?
> W. F. B. Yes, I like it to go through and think it will be a great advantage – very pleasant. There is a balcony with a way through in two places.

I had thought of putting a door through a bedroom wall to a large sleeping balcony. The same bedroom has another door on to a small balcony.

W. F. B. Outside the house, did you get the idea there should be something jutting out a little more – not the balcony? Though I couldn't see it, I feel 'Yes, it's right.'

A porch was built – the builder was submitting plans.

W. F. B. Won't you need to have a path improved – made harder? Later you'll see what I mean.

This I had not thought of, but when making the sunk garden I used the extra stone to make a wide paving outside the lounge door.

W. F. B. Walking down from this house you come to water.
F. E. B. Do you mean a pond or lake?
W. F. B. No – flowing water: you cannot see it from the house, but it's there and I like it; but I wouldn't want it too close so that you could see it.

The ground slopes down from the garden to the level of the river at Cookham. The Cliveden woods are on the horizon and the river flows between but is not visible from the house.

W. F. B. I like the church there. Not an old one, a modern one, has been restored, but part of the original building is still there. There is a field or grassy place beside it – not in the church grounds; I walked round and felt on grass; you might notice.
Near where the church is the road winds a bit and is not quite flat near the church.
There is a very tall hedge near, a tall wild hedge; it looks like a clipped hedge but is really wild.

INTRODUCTORY NOTE

This is an accurate description.

W. F. B. The place near begins with C – a place I like.

Cookham Dean.

> I have here a very happy person who wants to send you a message of gratitude – affectionate gratitude. Someone who was not happy on Earth but had it in her to be very happy given the right conditions. I think I told you about her – a doctor on Earth; she worked and had been among the poor not long before she passed over – I think she was in the East End. E. was her name – I can't get the other name. I think I told you how helped she had been by your thought and she wanted to come for one moment to say 'Thank you' for trying to give the right impression of her condition and her actions – throwing your weight on the side of fairness and justice to one who could not answer for herself.
> A. has been very helpful: she wanted to help her for your sake, but there is another link. A. and she had a mutual acquaintance, and also there was an institution in which A. had been interested and E. also with which you are not connected, but you may see someone who will give you a clue.

These links were quite unknown to me. E was the initial of the Christian name of the friend, and it seemed most unlikely that there should be any common ground between E. and Ada; but when I asked M.G., Ada's friend, if there could be any truth in it, she explained as follows. The mutual acquaintance was a medical missionary in India, a man of the same surname as E., who read a report of the Guild of the Handicapped and was so charmed by it that he asked to have it sent to him regularly, and hence a correspondence had begun between him and A.

Through another friend A. had subscribed to the Mission in which E. had been working, and so became interested in the work done.

W. F. B. They had a link therefore to talk about a person they both knew, and a work both were interested in. E. is *very* sympathetic, very sensitive, and has progressed very quickly since she passed over. Warmheartedness, zeal, sympathy hurried her towards her premature physical end. She died from what we might call sudden disease of the mind – on Earth called by another name. Her body was tired, her mind too, so she died from illness as truly as anyone who dies from consumption or cancer.

An individual living in a physical body can open himself to impressions from three quarters:

(1) From our side – deliberate, definite suggestion or advice from our side – the spirit realm.

(2) Suggestions picked up haphazard from the ether around him, which may be correct or incorrect – like listening on a telephone when the lines cross and you pick up conversations that have nothing to do with you, or by setting up conditions in which it is possible to receive the message.

(3) A message can be received through one's own higher self.

I should say with regard to mundane matters it would be better to rely on the promptings of one's own higher self than to ask help from ours, except when you may be doing something connected with us or which had a bearing on people or places connected with us on which you feel we should have a word if possible. Even then it is well to develop your own powers of discrimination, discretion and intuition, rather than seeking to draw upon ours – that is your way of development.

I'm afraid that many people who believe in what we call Spiritualism live and lean on their communications, never developing their own powers of perception or determination. Such a course is definitely wrong, and it is only permissible to be guided by us when you are carrying out a point in regard to which you want to be sure that you are carrying out something in accordance with our wishes.

INTRODUCTORY NOTE

What I mean briefly is, when you are working on a matter which affects us, it is permissible to ask our help, but even in that and in all other things develop your own judgment in dealing with things on your own plane: the more you do so, the more we are allowed to help you.
God helps those who help themselves – there is a lot of truth in it. God only allows us to help those who help themselves. Communication is always permissible so long as it is not allowed to interfere with the spiritual, the mental and physical development of the individual while on Earth.

* * * * * *

W. F. B. These are only silly little things, but I saw you doing them.
Did you have some paper stamped? I got the thought in connection with myself. You linked me in your mind with paper and stamping.

The week before I was ordering notepaper and came across his dies, which I had not used before.

W. F. B. Country *house:* Has something been held up or delayed? Don't be disappointed if you hear: it may only be a tiny delay, but it won't be quite right as soon as you thought.

Quite true – there were builders delays, which I discovered later.

W. F. B. I have a peculiar feeling about this; am looking forward to it more than anything you've undertaken since I passed over.
F. E. B. Anything important?
W. F. B. There doesn't seem to be, but I have a happy feeling about the house: I am going to like it.
While you're there interesting things will happen, though I don't know details. I shall be there a good deal from now on.

I am going to help to consecrate it with an element which will help me to be there and to let you know I am when you're there.

When later I went to the house my cook-house-keeper was helping to settle in. She had stayed with us at Carrigoona in Ireland. She came to me and said, 'Do you know it's so odd, but this place feels to me just like Carrigoona though it's not at all like it; but it feels as though Sir William were here.' She was a matter-of-fact woman, utterly unacquainted with psychic things.

W. F. B. God bless you, my dear. I am coming with you and shall be with you the rest of the day and this evening.

I was speaking at a meeting that evening.

June 30, 1930
Leonard Sitting

W. F. B. I have felt recently that the time will come when I shall be even more closely associated with you because I feel we have work to do together, apart from the sittings, apart from anyone else's work, we have something to do together. I do not know the details, but all you are doing now will be a foundation for it; your own work, your life with me, your investigations into the realms of psychical science both before and after my passing, will be of use to you in the work. It has all been groundwork and I shall be with you, working with you, impressing you when the time comes. Of course you know, don't you, that all depends on your will, your wish to co-operate, and upon your using ordinary common sense and methods of protecting yourself so that you will be here on Earth ready for the work.
I want you over here, but I must if possible help you to stay on the Earth for some years longer for the work only.
F. E. B. When will this work begin?

W. F. B. You will know, it will come and will be so obvious you will find yourself taking it and doing it, and then you will realise it is the work of which I told you in these sittings. The reason I want you now to go slowly, not to be hemmed in by work, especially routine work, is because I feel you must be ready, your brain and mentality rested and fresh so as to cope with the new order of things when it comes.

F. E. B. Are things on your side really as you thought they would be?

W. F. B. *Very* much. And do you remember I thought it would be governed very much by mind and we little understood the powers of the mind; therefore the conditions on this side are *very* different for different people. You're relegated to different planes according to your different outlook and capacity.

F. E. B. Shall I then be able to join you on your plane?

W.F.B. *Of course* you will, my darling; that is an absurd question. We are working together; we love each other; that alone gives us the right to be together and to work together. I can help you if you need it, but we do belong to the same plane. I know more of this side, naturally. If you had been to Yokohama and I had not, you would be in a superior position in some ways. But if I joined you in Yokohama you would instruct me and point out the conditions of life there, you would be able to go straight to a place to which I must find my way, and so you can be with me when you arrive on this side. But the conditions here seem to be very similar to those on Earth; do you understand what I mean? – the same *appearance*, but instead of being governed and influenced by your surroundings to such a great extent as you are, we have to learn to manipulate and control our surroundings, and the only preparation for that is that one must learn to use one's mind and control it experimentally on your side on the material things around us while we are still on Earth. People who have not learned to use their minds on Earth are at a terrible disadvantage on our side.

* * * * * *

W. F. B. Under the influence of an anaesthetic one's etheric body becomes separated from the physical one.

You are not completely anaesthetised unless the etheric body has been separated by the anaesthetic sleep, or a great shock may separate. Death always separates. An anaesthetic does separate, but if too great or too sudden, results in death.

F. E. B. Is it possible that when the etheric body is almost separated by an anaesthetic another entity may take possession of it?

W. F. B. It is *possible,* it does happen, it could do so with certain people. With some people it could not happen, but I believe it *has* happened with disastrous results.

If you show me a person whose physical and spiritual lives have been interwoven so that one is a part of the other, so that the mind and body cannot act in any way that is antipathetic to the soul or spirit, that person is safe under an anaesthetic from any invasion by an alien entity. I do not mean such persons are immune from physical disturbance; they may be the worst subjects of all for anaesthesia, but they are immune and safe from spiritual danger or interference.

CHAPTER 13

October 27, 1930
Leonard Sitting

Being unable to go to this sitting for professional reasons, it occurred to me that some message might be given if my secretary went instead. I therefore telephoned at 10:00 p.m. the evening before the sitting asking her to go next morning.

Later I remembered there were three messages I had specially wanted to get – two for friends and one for myself. 'Olive' had asked if I could get a message from her husband; Mrs. W. if I could get a further message from George; and I hoped to hear if W. F. B. had been in touch with my brother who had died recently.

This time, therefore, I used the method recommended by Myers – viz. to speak aloud in one's own room at home asking that the messages desired might if possible be given.

> W. F. B. Will you tell my wife I was with her yesterday very specially, she was talking to me last night; she was speaking to me aloud and I tried to answer her but could not do so, but I know she felt me, she sensed my presence very strongly several times yesterday.
> Will you ask her if she was counting money on Sunday? She seemed to be doing some particular calculations yesterday with regard to money matters.

I had been doing some accounts on the Sunday unknown to my secretary, who was not in the house.

> W. F. B. And will you ask her also whether she was reminded of me by something she was reading yesterday. She was thinking very much about me yesterday morning; she was thinking of the day I passed over, I felt her thinking of the day I passed over very strongly. Things she had been doing and thinking about had reminded her of the whole circumstances.

This is true.

> W. F. B. Ada is with me, and will you please say that Ada has now got an old friend with her, a lady of whom she was very fond when she was here. She was connected with a building in which Ada was interested when she was here. This lady knew all about Ada's work. They had been associated for many years, and Ada has been very pleased to welcome her. She has been an active and energetic woman all her life, but she had been in very bad health for the last two or three years, so Ada was not surprised to see her. I think the letter M has got something to do with her, M or N. And though she has not been at all in good health for two or three years she had kept an unselfish interest in things and in other people. She was an intensely good woman here and did a great deal of good. She will be helping Ada in the Children's Home she superintends.

This accurately describes a friend of Ada's whose name began with N.

> W. F. B. I wanted to ask her if she remembers the last time she went to speak to Whitehawk I told her she had psychic power herself, and I think I spoke to her about healing power. Apart from her own knowledge of surgery and medicine she has certainly a power of healing.

INTRODUCTORY NOTE

> Will you tell her that the houses and places do not matter to me now in the way they did here, but she has been thinking over things and wondering whether she may have to make changes, not immediate ones altogether, but possible changes in the future; I want to say to her, 'Do whatever you think best, don't consider what you think I should have liked when I was here on Earth, because my passing over has changed conditions and circumstances.' I want her to do everything now in the best way according to present conditions. Had I been alive in the physical body now things would have been different, certain changes would not have occurred, nor would they be likely to occur as long as I was in the body with her; but it is different now, so I want her to act as she thinks best. Will you tell her that I knew she had been looking at some old papers of mine recently. I knew she was thinking of them, and it was reminding her of my work on Earth about thirty years ago. I would like you to remind her of this; I am sure I am right in regard to the time.
> I am very glad you have come today, because I feel certain there are several things which you would not know about, but which my wife knows, and therefore it will in some ways be more evidential than if she had come herself.
> Olive; I have not seen Olive for a long time.

The name of one for whom I asked a message. Here followed a discussion with friends of my secretary, evidential to her.

> W. F. B. While I was waiting to think of something about Olive (i.e. that he was asked to do regarding Olive) they popped in. I wanted to say that I have been helping George; George has been with me a great deal; he has been working very hard with his wife.

George was the husband of the second friend for whom I asked a message.

W. F. B. Did my wife want to give some books of mine away? She has been thinking of my books again and was wondering what she had better do with them.

Yes. I had discovered a box of books not seen before.

W. F. B. I do not mind, tell her, do what she likes with the books. But I think that she was thinking of presenting them or giving them to something quite recently. Tell her it will be all right, I know they will be made good use of.
She was also thinking about some books of mine in a rather different way, on psychical subjects, survival and personality, but I cannot get her thought about them very clearly, but I knew that she was either reading or particularly interested in a book which was rather large and heavy and dealt with survival and personality. This was, I think, a few days ago.

I had been reading again the single volume of Myers' *Human Personality*.

W. F. B. Will you also tell her that it was very interesting to me to go again to old conditions with her, to be reminded again of years gone by and old friends and places.

The week before I had occasion to drive into the country by a route often driven with him, crossing the Wey at Weybridge.

W. F. B. It was not in London, we were some distance from London; the surrounding conditions were of the country, and I think of water too. I could not see the water but I was conscious of it. Tell her I cannot always see everything round her, but that sometimes, as on this occasion, I get a general idea of the locality.
And please also remind her of this, the little box. Just say this to her, 'The little box, the one I always kept near me.' I know she was reminded of it and thinking of the little box. I did

speak to her about the little box some time ago, in fact a long time ago in a sitting, but lately she has been thinking of it. She was thinking of something rather special about a photograph of me lately. She wanted to put a photograph of me in a new place. It is as if she were going to put it in a place where there was not one before. I only wanted her to know that I knew she was thinking of it, that was all.

I had taken one of his photographs to the country.

W. F. B. There is not a great deal of power, but I have got through most of the things that I wanted to say.
Tell her I am helping her, and that I cannot see ahead for everything, but I am allowed to help her.
W. F. B. I don't see everyone who comes over to this side because I knew them or was related to them on Earth. People pass over and the ignorant section of the world would expect me to see them as a matter of course, but that is not so. When you come I shall be with you *at once*. I shall lie with you before you leave your body and immediately we shall be together.
Oh! *darling*, why did you think about my shoes or slippers lately? I could not see but felt your thoughts.

The week before I had gone to the drawer in which was his court suit and found some shoes.

W. F. B. Did you see a pair I had had some time previous to passing over? And, darling, what did you think with regard to something special I drank out of? You will remember a bottle, you were reminded about it.

An old flask he used to take to Carrigoona with him. I found it recently.
The following message clearly relates to my brother. It was the third message asked for in my room at home the night before my secretary took the sitting for me on October 30, 1930.

W. F. B. I have a man with me who has just come over lately, a man you have known a very long while, but you have not been with him so much lately. The letter B is there all the time he is talking. He is not a boy, he is getting on in years. He has a tired feeling, but he had not been well for a considerable time.

Bristol was his home.
His age was 69.
He had been ill for some time though going about.

W. F. B. I have been helping him because he was a little surprised and amazed at some of the conditions here.
He knew who I was, but did not quite realise why I was there. He kept on saying 'But you are dead, you are dead, you are dead,' and thought he was dreaming.

This was said exactly as my brother might have said it.

W. F. B. He informed me I was dead two or three times. I did not argue with him *at that stage*, it was not worthwhile; I waited till he had seen some more people who were also what he called dead. Then he began to realise that he was not dreaming about so many people or for such a long period of time.
He is not with me – that is to say he does not live with me, but I have seen him. He is happier now.
F. E. B. Was he not happy at first?
W. F. B. No, it was a difficult condition for him: he could not adjust himself mentally; he was worried before he passed over; I think he exaggerated, things were out of perspective, he could not mentally adjust himself before he left the Earth, his mental condition at the time of passing was not very good.

He was under the influence of morphia for acute pain.

INTRODUCTORY NOTE

F. E. B. Did he meet friends he knew at once?
W.F.B. Yes, but not those. He has a lady with him, a young lady.
F. E. B. Who?
W. F. B. Not Ada; someone related who passed over some time before. She is young; he is happy with them.

Violet, his daughter, and 'them' probably refers to his first wife, who died years before: she was Violet's mother.

W.F.B. When you think about it he had several people on this side he loved, three specially near him. There is a man friend with a J in his name, passed over not long before.

J. was the son of an old friend while on Earth. He had asked me to try to get in touch with J. for his parents' sake, but it was not very successful.

W.F.B. M is a letter connected with him, not the M. on Earth, someone passed over. And E. is someone passed over a long time; she is near him.

? Elizabeth, his mother?

F. E. B. Tell me who he is – you have not told me his name.
W. F. B. He has been away from where you live for a long time. But you know he had rather a long illness some time before he passed over and he had got better in some ways, but did not quite recover. You would think of him more as you knew him some time ago. He is interested in you, but his principal memories are of some time ago.

True. I had seen very little of him for some years as he rarely came to London.

W. F. B. I do not think you and he would agree about everything; you have different personalities and temperaments.

Though a nice man he was a bit difficult, not always easy to get on with. He would wish to be kind and good, but there were little kinks in his mentality which made him at times a little difficult for himself.

That is very characteristic.

W. F. B. He is finding it difficult now, adjusting himself to other people, to other ideas as well as his own. He is learning to do it and he is therefore happier, but it has been an effort. This man knew something about this subject, yet he did not apply it in the same way that I did.

This is true: it interested him, but he never studied the subject.

W. F. B. The knowledge had helped me, and in a little while when he has adjusted himself more he will be very happy indeed. He was interested in something to do with churches, not parsons but religion.
He wanted to write something before he passed over and did not do it. There is something he feels he ought to have written to do with arranging material affairs, making something right for a person on Earth, things he ought to have done. He is thinking about a man too, a youngish man, and he has been anxious about him. He has not been very satisfied about some arrangement connected with these people. It is his own fault, but he did not look into things, not as he thinks he ought to have done.
Things made it difficult for him, the conditions round him made it difficult. He is doing his best to help, but not finding it easy now to adjust the material conditions, but he is trying to.

I did not know to what this referred, but on enquiry found that he had meant to alter some financial arrangements.

W. F. B. Will you be seeing or hearing of these people soon? I have brought him today so that you may be able to do

INTRODUCTORY NOTE

something to a third person you will be in touch with soon. He is doing all he can to adjust matters; things have been held up since his passing.

I saw his wife by chance shortly after this sitting and from her had an explanation of all this.

W. F. B. Why does Ada think now about war? At the time of the Great War she had it on her mind very much; others scarcely noticed it in comparison. With her it mattered in a big sense.

She was a strong pacifist and the war was a constant misery to her. She suffered with all who suffered.

F. E. B. She was quite right really.
ADA. Yes, dear, I know I was. I stood alone and it was not very comfortable and easy at the time.
F. E. B. You were very brave and true.
ADA. I was true to what I thought was right, and now I find I was right. I knew I was at the time, but my views were not popular. I find I am right now, but not one in a hundred agreed with me then. Some thought it, but were cowards and would not say so.
W. F. B. One thing, Ada always sticks to her guns.
ADA. Do you remember my holding forth at first and then I closed up and quietened a little? There were times when I felt I ought to speak, but it was not any good. I work for peace now. You knew I was right, but did not see what other course was open to the country. I say any course, but not murder.

Very true and typical.

W. F. B. She is very firm, she won't take a word back, you can't move her.
It may interest you to know Ada is considered to be a leader,

a thinker and a teacher on this side. She knew the truth; she stands for it.

I did my best to send messages last time, but it was not quite the same as talking to you.

CHAPTER 14

March 30, 1931
Leonard Sitting

W. F. B. I think it's intended that when you reach a certain point in your evolution you have to depend on our side, the spiritual side, for help. You can help others, *but* for yourself you have to turn to our side.
Our Lord can help you. I can only help you through *His help and love*. I have seen Him, have spoken to Him, and I am going again to see Him this Easter, when I know you will be thinking of Him and me.
He wants you to think of him as a great friend, the greatest friend of all. The first time I saw Him I realised that it was the culmination of all that I had hoped for and believed in. He was the greatest demonstrator of these very truths that we are trying to explain to poor misguided humanity today. I shall see Him again at Easter.
F. E. B. Can you get in touch with Him whenever you wish?
W. F. B. Yes, but that would be mentally. If I wish guidance or inspiration I raise myself mentally in aspiration to Him. My body does not move, but my spirit (which is not my body) goes to Him and my thoughts register what He tells my spirit on to my etheric brain. When you pray, your spirit reaches

out to Our Lord and brings back something from Him; very often your brain is charged with the returning power and love that the spirit has brought back with it. That is the reason that peace often follows prayer; a curious solution of difficulties often comes after prayer.
You ask me whether I can communicate with Him whenever I like. I cannot go to Him in my present body, but I am more conscious of His replies, the thought that comes back, and the inspiration, more than one could on Earth.

* * * * * *

W. F. B. My body of course is not the same as it was, yet it is a body of substance: not the substance you could handle with the present substance of your hand: the whole thing is a matter of adjustment. Now I'm standing close to you. If you put your hand out you would put it through me because your substance is not adjusted to mine. We are rather like light in that respect: one ray crossing and interpenetrating another. How glad I shall be when you can leave this very difficult world and join us here in the new life – the perfect life. In a few years when we are together again the whole of our lives on Earth will seem to be a very short page in the book of life.
ADA. When I look back on mine it did seem short – too short. I could hardly believe it when it dawned on me my time on earth might be drawing to a close. You remember those days I suppose; you realise I didn't altogether take in to myself the realisation that I was definitely going to leave the earth. The idea had come to me, but I thought, 'No, there are things to do'; I didn't really think I was going to leave the Earth so soon.

She was taken suddenly ill in the midst of busy preparations for Christmas gifts and entertainment for her Guild of the Handicapped, but did not think she was dying till the very end.

INTRODUCTORY NOTE

W. F. B. I see Sydney sometimes. Sydney has been helping the other one since he passed over – he's helping him to adjust himself.

Sydney was a brother who died many years ago – he was closely related to A., his brother, who was one and a half years older. In boyhood they were always together.

W. F. B. A. is quite happy and likes the life, but didn't know much about it and needed to be adjusted. He had so many good points that balanced the blank spaces.
He'll develop and help others now.
A. wants to speak about Brian – he wanted to help Brian and M. Is there some anxious, troubled condition round them? As if several on the other side were trying to get together to lift it.

Brian and Michael were his two grandsons.

W. F. B. I'm often with you. I'm so near you. When I come to Earth I can't go everywhere; there are very few links I can use on Earth.
It's such a peculiar idea. On Earth we think we've got ties of relationship – even if people worry us we think it a duty to be with them. The only real ties we have to consider on my side are the ties of love nothing. We are taught to cling to whoever will lead us in the right direction.
You and I found the right way together more than we ever found apart. Our association opened up many new ways that all led in the right direction.
I am so thankful that I knew about this great truth so that we could go into it together. I led you into this a good deal, but you aided and abetted me.
ADA. And I was so glad when you came here and I could speak to you – so glad – so glad.
W. F. B. But it isn't just speaking to you here. Really I am able to help you in what may be a rather intangible way.

Sometimes, though you don't know it comes from me, you feel the help. It's in those ways where no one on Earth can help we come in.

May 29, 1931. (M.W. present with F. E. B.)
Leonard Sitting

> W. F. B. I have been with you lately and very close to you indeed.
> George is also very pleased and sends his love to his wife.
> George: (speaking to his wife.) I want you to understand the prayers and thoughts that you have been sending out to and for me have helped me more than I can possibly tell you.
> You have helped me more than you will know until you reach this side and we are together again.
> I have been helping Alfred. There are several now because he needs it. Not what you call physical bodily help, but mental help.

Alfred is Ada's brother who has passed over, never mentioned in a Leonard Sitting since his death, though Ada sent a message to him in life.

> George: I don't want to come back to earth. I am free in mind and body; I don't want to come into the physical body again, but to come back to you in a spiritual way. I don't even want to come back to you in any material way. The higher the way the better for both. We can live together on a plane where I can meet you, where I do not descend to you, but you ascend to me; your thoughts help you to live on that plane.
> W. F. B. Every day we see one person meeting another, reunion, that is why we are happy. People think 'How can they be happy when they see us broken with grief?' We are happy because we are constantly seeing reunions between those who have been parted, and when they rejoin it seems

as though it had only been a day. When you meet them on this side you will realise all eternity before, so therefore a few years on earth seems so little looking back.
George: What have you been doing with my case? You were looking at it.

This leather case had been seen and described by Miss Bazett on March 12, when she saw George W. (not at a sitting) and gave messages from him.

W. F. B. I want you to know I am and have been helping you with conditions on your side. I am glad you are having the sitting now. I do not forget the anniversaries and I have been thinking; but when these times come round I try to prevent your thinking of the physical aspect of my passing, only that I was released from a body that held me, and set free to enter the healthy, robust spiritual body.

May 26 was the date of his passing in 1925.

W. F. B. I want you to do something I have told you on previous occasions. Postpone definite decisions and taking definite steps up to the last moment, up to the last reasonable moment in regard to what relates to your work and places; in your life one reacts on the other. About postponing, do not run the risk of leaving a thing too late, but reasonably late. I am always afraid of appearing to exaggerate and making you think you can leave a thing so late that there is danger of losing something.
F. E. B. I do not understand what you are talking about.
W. F. B. Yes, but you will. If there is anything to decide don't do it before you need.
There is every day a possibility of something occurring which might make you alter a decision – you will understand.

This proved to be very true. Had I given up my country cottage I should not have been able to have my sister with me in the last year of her life.

> W. F. B. I am helping you to reconstruct life and put it on a suitable and easy basis with as little worry as possible.
> I want you to do the most you can while you are here.
> I will do everything to help you to go on quietly and carefully as you usually do. You might get mixed up with somebody else's troubles: they are round you now, not yours. I never want you to turn your back on things, which is so easy. I am going to help you to tackle it, but yet I want to say you cannot carry people, it is not right to ask people to take difficulties for them. It is difficult for you to see how far you ought to go and how far not. It looks like being caught in something troublesome. But there is a reason for your being drawn in, a purpose.
> This is in higher hands than mine.

This proved to be very true. The troubles of friends made it very necessary for me to share them.

> W. F. B. Today you are what is called between things, there is so much developing, so much I have got to help you to see through, but I can and will help.
> We are sometimes told never to give advice of that kind to people on Earth because they lean on us too much and may lead to leaving responsibility and choice to us.
> We are both very fortunate in that way in being able to collaborate with those we loved best on Earth.
> I feel so sorry for those who long to help and cannot because the Earth lives are closed to them.
> Whatever my plans are for you I never want you to be submerged. No alliance or friendship that would hamper you. In spite of friends you are sometimes rather lonely, but a free loneliness is better than a limiting companionship. You were

free with me. I never fussed you; I never forced suggestions. Our companionship suited you. You knew I was so interested. You suited me too, you helped me so.

It was a wonderful companionship that few would have understood.

W. F. B. You know, don't you, dear, that I want to work with you and there is so much material I have. I'll leave it to you to arrange when you can. It is better for us not to dictate; your world is no longer mine.

Don't think for a moment the future is going to be less busy and less interesting. It will be more interesting than it's ever been, not such a grind of uninteresting things and happenings, but all opening out, a development of activities on an interesting plane.

You know, since I've been on this side I've found that you have a curious mixture of feelings about people. You like to meet and come in touch with them, but you like to feel, 'I can be free and alone again when it is necessary.' I don't want you to be lonely, but I want you to be alone when it's right. You couldn't live unless you did. It would dry up something in you, use up something.

Not when you were with me – that was quite different. Something in you missed me even more than your closest friends understand. You were alone with me and yet you had company with me.

There has been a vacuum in your life which you have endeavoured to fill since I passed and yet you've known you couldn't quite fill it. You see there is no one in your life now who could live with you and yet leave you alone and yet not lonely. There is a great difference in being able to be alone without being lonely, and that is how you were with me.

George was pleased with his talk and asks me to thank you for letting him have the talk. He wants to help more and loves to keep a close link.

He thinks that he will be able to get more in touch with his wife now. He has been in touch and impressing her more than

he would have thought possible. He says, 'She is closer to me.'
I am enjoying my life more than I ever thought possible, more than I ever dreamed. I'm enjoying every moment of my day, if one can call it a day when there is no night.

You know how I should like you to be with me, so that we could go together to see interesting places which did exist and are apparently lost – Ancient Egypt.

Do you remember my speaking to you about Atlantis? I can visit those places now as they were. When a place lives it lives as it were at its best.

F. E. B. Then can you go back in time?

W. F. B. No, the place exists as it was, and the people not as they were but in style as they lived, but with new additional knowledge.

The Earth is round like a ball. Spheres are round the Earth like a circumference and larger. Each country on Earth has its duplicate on the sphere above it. England is more or less immediately over England on the Earth, Egypt over Egypt of the present day; but it does not necessarily take its form, shape, details or colour from the Egypt of today. It takes it from the old Egypt at its best.

Places and people live at their best on our side, whether 5,000 years ago or last month or week.

The zenith is the time in which a person or place lives on our side.

You remember when I was on Earth I was very interested in these bygone glories – Rome before its collapse, Atlantis and Egypt.

It is so interesting to see them as they were, inhabited by people who knew and loved and lived in them, but who have gained special experience they had not on Earth. In fact each of these great empires had a fall, a collapse which was entirely due to lack of spirituality in the life of the people. They worked up to a point of physical, material excellence, even artistic excellence of which we have proof in plenty, but as they eliminated either spiritual knowledge or observance of spiritual laws they collapsed, and so should we collapse today, and so would all those who do not live in accordance with the spiritual law. By spiritual law I don't mean a narrow orthodox religion, but according to divine love and order and understanding.

Spain and Italy are two countries bound to have trouble. I have greater hope in England than in any other nation, and I myself belong to a band, a society, who are endeavouring to help this country to find itself spiritually, and before you pass over (I'm afraid a few years yet) you will have found a way to spread spiritual knowledge on the Earth. I was glad I had been allowed to do something myself.

But through you I shall do more because through you I shall make people more conscious of this other world, and that everyone must be prepared for it, so they had better understand the geography of it. I want you to help them to do that, but do that in your own time when you are more settled.

You are not quite settled yet, but you're becoming more settled. You have a good deal of medical work still to do, you cannot drop that, but you are freer; it is possible to keep time and opportunity for other things and yet time to relax as well. Nature and fresh air are so important to you.

CHAPTER 15

October 30, 1931
Leonard Sitting

W. F. B. Do you remember when I first passed over I told you there would come to Earth a very important period, that I and many others were preparing for it? That time has come: we have now entered on a very important period indeed. There are difficulties ahead, very grave difficulties: I want you to know I am helping; I shall be very close indeed to you from now onwards because my work is in the Earth conditions and will be for some time. I shall be able to help and impress you more than I have ever done. I want you to get into the habit of opening your mind to me when you go to bed, and then you will find that I shall impress you with the right solution to your difficulties in the morning.
Talk to me at night before you go to sleep, quietly, passively, setting your problems into simple language.
Definite thought – don't think round a subject, focus on it as plainly as possible.
What will happen will be while your body is asleep your mind will co-operate with mine and retain the solution that we shall have arrived at together. On waking in the morning,

as soon as you begin to think of the troublesome subject you will find the solution to it presents itself – inserts itself . . .

F. E. B. Resolves itself?

W. F. B. . . . *inserts* itself into your physical brain just as a clear, definite idea does. Get into the habit of it – it will be very helpful.

I want to be near you and help you. You know I love you. I did and do. There is no one else on Earth who can help, advise and love you as much as I do. Everything you are undertaking and planning is a step in the right direction.

F. E. B. What do you mean?

Things you have in your mind to have done – in regard to the house in the country – they are all steps in the right direction. Though there will be a period of great difficulty in this country you will be safe; your condition, your position, everything will be safe.

F. E. B. I am not afraid.

W. F. B. I did not think you would be. I only wanted to tell you what I thought.

There will be a new interest for you – new friends soon. You have been feeling as if you wanted some fresh atmosphere in the way of interest, friends, work. Your mind is seeking for more scope.

Ada said to me a while ago that your mind rebelled against narrowness more than ever and will. What happens now for you must all be in a wider field; you must not be tied down too much either to narrow people or conditions. The time has come when you need breadth and depth and the shallow waters have grown stagnant, as shallow waters do in time.

I am entering deeper waters, wider spheres myself. Recently I have had what you would call a great development and feel that you will share it in some measure on Earth. I have been to other spheres attending lectures, courses of instruction on higher spheres than my own, the result of an experience and development of minds that belong to great ones of the past. I have had the benefit of their experience on both planes and also of the philosophy which became theirs through that experience.

I want to help you when I have gathered more information. I am able to use a certain amount of what I learn on these higher spheres on my own plane, but I can't always tell it to you. But I gain additional power through my knowledge with which I can help you, though I cannot always explain it to you. There will be further developments towards the East which will involve England.

F. E. B. Will there be wars?

W. F. B. Not a great war. I think we shall keep out, but there'll be great anxiety; warfare of a kind without meaning war for England.

There will be trouble but light ahead. We shall pull through, but it will be difficult while we are doing it.

February 15, 1932
Leonard Sitting

W. F. B. Last time you remember I told you this country has entered a very important period – I told you it would not so long ago.

Now I feel there are new channels into which your work and activities will be guided. For that reason I wanted you to have a comparatively quieter time.

F. E. B. What is the work?

W. F. B. It is the combination of the knowledge and study you've already had, and new ideas you will be given from my side. I feel it will be connected with your own work, connected with the spiritual and mental side of health. This thing called life with all your knowledge on Earth you don't know its composition. You only know what it does, its expression, because its source is not on or in the physical plane. It is very difficult to trace a thing which has not its source or origin in the physical. These you have to come to our side to trace.

As I told you before, life does not flow immediately into the physical body: it has an intermediate channel through which it must pass before it can animate the physical. This intermediate state or channel is called the etheric body, and we know when so-called death takes place the etheric body is drawn from the physical, and the latter being deprived of its channel through which it obtained its only real sustenance, crumbles and decays. The soul has departed, we say.

Literally that is true, but in what has it departed, what is its vehicle? Because the soul and spirit need a means of expression, a channel, or they are inactive, impotent. Well, the natural body for the soul is the etheric body: the physical was only the secondary one – what you might call the secondary impression, the shadow of the substance.

So many of us on the Earth have got into the habit of calling and thinking of the physical body as the substance, the real body, but it is the etheric body that is the real body, the physical is only a temporary manifestation of the etheric and of its powers.

Spirit, mind and matter – we cannot dissociate any of these. When the physical becomes dissociated it means death – an end to it.

Perfect health is only attained and kept by a perfect balancing and consciousness of the three states.

George is here and he sends his love to you. Did you know George has seen and welcomed someone who has passed recently? George is here and the lady is here.

F. E. B. Would the lady speak to me?

W. F. B. They are both trying to help the other one. The lady knows she is going to be very happy here.

She was very tired for some time and she was extremely glad to be rid of the physical body; it was extraordinary that she had so much vitality as she had under the circumstances.

M. W.'s sister had recently passed over after a very short illness and heart failure.

INTRODUCTORY NOTE

F. E. B. What was her name?
W. F. B. There is something about a letter connected with her. George was with her before she left the body, helping her. Mm, Mady, *Muddy*.

Muddy was the name her sister called her.

W. F. B. She doesn't quite understand conditions yet. I told her to come.
There's one on Earth she wants to help and I'm trying to help. George helps as well, but Muddy wants to help too, and they feel the one on Earth is thinking of them both, and how strange that they have met and are together, leaving the one here.
The one here is not very well – better, but not really as well as she ought to be even now. She gets very tired of things – weary of them. She's had a difficult life, specially the last few years.
F. E. B. Is there a message from George?
W. F. B. Specially that he has met this one and is looking after her. There are other people here too near to her who knew her long ago. Her mother is very devoted to her and so pleased to meet her again after this long time. As well as Muddy another name, M.
Control: When he was speaking a spirit form of a gentleman – rather tall, well built – darkish, elderly, rather good features, rather on the big side. He stands near George and Muddy.

Mrs. W.'s father, whose Christian name began with M, had passed over not long before the sister.

W. F. B. He belongs; he's interested in you and is pleased to speak to you.

I had known him from childhood.

W. F. B. They are all thinking how happy when the other one passes over. She has not a great deal to live for and they will be pleased to see her, and she them. She thinks about it and it will all be so natural when the time comes. They all send love to you.

ADA. We invited them to come today because we knew you'd be pleased to hear about Muddy, but we two, Will and I, *are your special ones*. No one comes nearer to you in the world than we do.

F. E. B. Is there a stranger there I wanted you to help?

W. F. B. Yes, a man passed over lately, rather suddenly. I was sorry for him and have tried to help him because I knew he wouldn't be very happy when he first arrived. W connected with him.

Initial of his Christian name.

He knew a little about our side but hadn't pursued it. He has got a brain and he'll use it and soon know what conditions are here. He is so sorry for her.

F. E. B. Is there a message for her?

W. F. B. Not today. Some time I'll bring one when he's more used to it. Something she'll know and understand. You felt sorry for her. It all seems so disappointing to her – abrupt ending. Though you don't know her you've a round link with her. I know you'll be able to help her – we'll do it. Writing, writing – not automatic, to do with the man. Writing left behind.

This man whom I had asked W. F. B. to find if possible had died very suddenly on a journey. There were some manuscripts of his lost which were subsequently found. They had been left behind in Europe. I knew nothing of the loss of the manuscripts till I told his wife of this sitting.

CHAPTER 16

May 26, 1932
Leonard Sitting

> W. F. B. You know I'm with you and thinking of you at all times. There are very few moments when I'm not thinking of you.
> F. E. B. But you have other things to do.
> W. F. B. Yes, but thought of you runs through them. Even when I'm working and concentrating *you're there*. It struck me just recently, the thought of you is rather like a beam of light passing through glass. The thought is the light: the work I'm doing – tasks, occupations, pleasures – are the glass through which the thought filters – not interfering but passing through and illuminating all.
> Did you think of me in a church which reminded you of old times? I felt very near to you, as if I had got on to the same spiritual plane, as if we were very near together in the highest sense of the word.

I had been to the churchyard at Longcross to take flowers and stayed to the service in the church. It was the church we attended when living at Longcross House.

> W. F. B. I would very much like to carry out another book test. I made you think about this recently. The problem is to find a book you will not be accused of having read.
> I think I've got over that difficulty; there are plenty which you have not looked at lately – you haven't the time.
> I am showing you a room – it looks like the London house. I am going in at the door and I'm taking you to the right, and on the right against the wall are shelves. If you were going to walk round right from the door to a window, take the third shelf from the bottom, count the books from the door end.
> Take the fourth book from the door end: you open it at page 132. Will you see if on that page there is something to do with eyes or eyesight? And something which would apply to me, to my character, activities and endeavours when on Earth. 'Eyesight' has nothing to do with me, but a reference to eyesight or *vision* is given there.

'Vision' was spoken in direct voice, interrupting the words spoken by the Control.

> You will be more interested in the reference to character, temperament and activities. It is as if they described them on that page. I hope they won't sound as if I'd grown very conceited since I passed over. It is a serious book – a heavy work I may say.
> There is a certain amount of philosophy in it. It has an extraordinarily wide range of subject and period: even at the beginning of the book it speaks of things which happened many centuries ago. It speaks of foreign countries and their ways and customs. It was not published recently – a good many years ago – but page 132 is the most important page which will remind you of me.

The book was *A Short Sketch of English Literature*, by Professor Henry Morley.

INTRODUCTORY NOTE

On page 132 begins a paragraph on 'The Vision of Piers Plowman.'

'It is a vision of Christ seen through the clouds of humanity – a spiritual picture of the labour to maintain right and uphold the life spent upon duty done for the love of God.

'Everywhere it gives flesh and blood to its abstractions by the most vigorous directness of familiar detail so that every truth might, if possible, go home even by the cold hearthstone of the hungriest and most desolate of the poor to whom its words of a wide sympathy were recited.' The 'spiritual picture' is a very true description of the ideals by which W. F. B. strove to live.

The teaching of abstract principles by illustration drawn from the familiar things in life can be found illustrated in the writings of W. F. B. and in some of these scripts.

The first two chapters are on 'The forming of the people,' and the historical sketch ranges from 600 B.C. to A.D. 1066.

The following extract is one illustration of reference to foreign countries, their ways and customs:

> Once Europe was peopled only here and there by men who beat at the doors of nature and upon the heads of one another with sharp flints. What knowledge they struck out in many years was bettered by instruction from incoming tribes, who, beginning earlier and learning faster, brought higher results of experience out of some part of the region that we now call Asia. Generation after generation came and went, and then Europe was peopled by tribes different in temper: some scattered among pastures with their flocks and herds, or gathering for fight and plunder around chiefs upon whom they depended; others drawing together on the fields they ploughed, able to win and strong to hold the good land of the plain in battle under chiefs whose strength depended on them.

This book test was taken from shelves in a corner of the drawing-room from which Myers had given a book test through Mrs. Leonard when W. F. B. and I had been the sitters. It may interest readers unfamiliar with book tests if I record this one.

Myers said he had chosen the test from a room other than the study because we should be less familiar with the books.

He gave exact directions to find the book, which proved to be *Middlemarch,* by George Eliot. The two books adjoining, he said, contained much of W.F.B.'s work when a very young man.

They were Tyndall's *Light and Sound.* W. F. B. had assisted Tyndall in some of the experiments recorded.

The test was given on page 78 of *Middlemarch.*

Myers said, 'I want you to take the words at the top of this page as my answer to the question in your mind since I passed over.' They were, 'Ay, ay, I remember, I remember .'em all, every one.' In Myers' *Human Personality,* page 334, we read, 'What then is to be our conception of identity prolonged beyond the tomb? ... Do we ask that our friend or we should remember always or should remember all?'

> W. F. B. Do you know what I've got in my hand? That funny little blue flower you call forget-me-not. I bring it as a symbol of remembrance and also as a sign that I was with you when you were looking at them and speaking of them lately.

I had been looking at a new myosotis (heavenly blue) and thinking how he would have liked its vivid colour.

September 21, 1932
Leonard Sitting

> F. E. B. What are you doing now?
> W. F. B. I am still studying the new methods of establishing communication between the etheric and the physical bodies. Do you remember I told you before that I felt physical health and well-being depended on co-operation between the two bodies? I have learnt something more about this subject: that the etheric body which you have now can be the transmitter of health and strength, but also it can be the innocent vehicle or carrier of certain – let us call them – conditions which are

INTRODUCTORY NOTE

injurious or destructive in action on and in the physical body. The etheric body is not in any sense harmful in itself, but it is a carrier, and conductor; when it officiates as a carrier of spiritual influence or communication of mental influences from our side, or healing power from our side, it is a beneficent body, a beneficent channel, but there are so many active yet poisonous and destructive elements in the area of the Earth conditions which can be picked up and transferred through the etheric body, and you might say they gain in intensity and in their hostile pro-divides that they may definitely injure the physical body.

An example of that would be the destructive vibrations of extreme noise. Take shell-shock – we are apt to think of shell-shock in a crude sense as a terrific sound which has damaged the nerves of the patient through the sense of hearing. It is something more than that. The vibrations of noise pass through the etheric body and collect or carry with them into the physical system a certain amount of what I can only call poisonous matter in a fluidic state – invisible but none the less potent, as many destructive conditions are.

Most or many of the most destructive elements in your lives are invisible in themselves, and it is only the effects of them that become visible.

Take electricity – invisible in itself – visible or tangible to the ordinary senses through or by some mechanical device which renders it active in visible form. You have that to contend with; you also have noise, and you have waves set up by wireless apparatus. All these elements are disintegrating.

We must either adjust ourselves to them (at the present moment we don't see how to) or we must protect ourselves – which is the easier of the two, but it is the etheric body that is the carrier of these dangerous conditions. When the etheric body leaves the physical body to corruption at death, the physical body then becomes immune from any attack by these conditions. In the past we have rather loosely talked about death as a condition that leaves the physical body without feeling or consciousness. Something has ceased to function. What? Something that was there a moment ago, the next – it is not there. What is it? It is simply the withdrawal or separation of the etheric body which was the carrier of life to the physical body.

We cannot locate the seat of life in the physical because it is not there. How many have tried to find something in the physical organism – the seat of life – some spark, germ, cause of what is called life.

It doesn't lie in the physical body, it is useless looking for it there. It is in the etheric – or more correctly, the etheric is the true carrier of life.

It is the etheric body in which the soul lives, not in the physical. It animates it, influences it, and – moreover as important – it is influenced by the physical as long as the physical and the etheric are united.

The soul is appealed to, and influenced by the physical body through the senses.

How can we use it for health purposes? We have to learn to give the etheric body conditions which will be beneficial to the physical when carried through the etheric to the physical. Temporary isolation from destructive conditions.

You have an instinct very strongly for being alone at times. Not because you are bored with people, not because you're selfish, but some inner sense tells you it is necessary for your mental and physical welfare.

This is necessary for everybody, because the vibrations of another presence unless in perfect harmony are destructive and at times even dangerous to one's health. One wants to get away from noise, an instinct of self-preservation.

All human beings should be able to have peace and quiet, just as we expect to have fresh air, food, water and sleep, for the well-being of our physical health; but though we naturally demand our rightful dose of food and drink, we often forget that there are other conditions, excitement, noise, anxiety, and all the other more subtle and invisible elements which

INTRODUCTORY NOTE

make up life – thought currents, electricity, waves of different kinds. We have ignored these through ignorance, but they are to be reckoned with as much as the most obvious ones of eating and drinking.

A time in each day should be set apart by everyone for complete relaxation – not only of body but mind, and immunisation from the destructive elements such as noise and movement.

If you are sitting in a car in a medley of swirling traffic moving in different directions, both the noise and the contrary movement are bad.

How much easier going with the traffic is, on the same principle as floating with the stream – going with the current. Argument is the same; the clash of opinions, of wills, may be stimulating at times, but is destructive as a rule. In modern life there is so much that clashes, jars, fights, disintegrates.

I should say life is more destructive now in these strong though subtle ways than it has ever been, but the influence is ignored because the effect is not registered on the physical body, but through the nervous system.

We are working and studying – trying to bring influences to bear on people in the Earth life, who are able to provide facilities for this immunisation of which I have spoken. It is peace and relaxation that is necessary. If we can give those conditions we shall find there will be a better ground soil in our physical bodies. I look upon our physical bodies as ground soil that has to be tilled, fed and nourished and cared for by the etheric which is the soul body.

The quality of the soil and the state in which the soil can be kept determines the question as to whether the individual inhabits a healthy body or an unhealthy one. The soil is the breeding ground, the seed that goes in comes up true to type if the soil is right for it, whether good seed or bad; the germ of disease or the seed of health. It is the character of the soil that matters. The seed matters, but the bad seed is not likely to grow in a soil only suitable to healthy seed.

Seed of disease must have the soil that suits it. Unfortunately the conditions of which I spoke help to provide soil which is suitable as breeding ground for the seed or germ of disease. I consider it most important. In a few years what I am telling you now will be spoken of as a new discovery, and yet in line with orthodox research.

I know I am right about it.

We've only become aware of the visible conditions on the Earth, but the broadcasting and electrical power is teaching us to become aware of the invisible conditions round us. There are many more potent invisible conditions whose application we have yet to discover.

The next thing you on Earth will discover as a follow on to the wireless producing sound and vision, and electrical power producing heating and light, will be the power of movement – propelling power that can be drawn from the ether, or used from and in the ether in the same way that ether is made use of in broadcasting. There will be power of movement in a way hitherto unknown. You will hear of this before long, and you will say, 'This is the discovery of which he spoke.' We are trying to help these discoveries forward, but unfortunately we find it is easier to impress you with the importance of their usefulness than we find it to impress you with their danger and with the necessity of protecting and immunising yourselves against them.

You see that, my dear, don't you? You are all imbued with the advantages of electricity, but no one takes the trouble seriously to consider the disadvantages, because the advantages are so obvious.

I hope later to be able to tell you how to protect yourselves individually. I cannot at present; our investigations are incomplete. They are difficult because they concern your Earth conditions which are no longer ours. We operate in the ether, but we do not charge up chemically in the same way that you do. That is not necessary in our lives as we live in a world of finer matter than yours that is more easily operable by thought.

INTRODUCTORY NOTE

I have a certain feeling about a dog. Might he have to be moved for a time? He's fretting, he doesn't like being away from you. He is physically all right but lonely. Why is he not loose enough? Perhaps someone is afraid to let him loose. He is fretting, lonely and miserable and too much kept in. He's not very happy.

I did not know that my dog, Peko, had been kept under these conditions till after this message. The housekeeper had been keeping him tied up and only out on a lead. He had been under a vet for a month without improvement. I acted on this advice and brought him home to London and he was well in a week.

W. F. B. A dog's life is very circumscribed; not long, and every day seems longer than ours; they have nothing to do – a boring life, and we seldom think of it in that way.

CHAPTER 17

December 1, 1932
Leonard Sitting

W. F. B. But you want to know my life in my own conditions. If I were to take a typical day as you call it – I think of one quite recently in which were incorporated a good many happenings which can be explained in ordinary terms.
There are some things we can't tell you about, that are outside the range of your imagination. There are experiences one has – that if one tried to speak of them in ordinary language of Earth it would be impossible. My usual life is very similar to the life on Earth. I meet other people; I'm interested in science; I meet these exponents of science and we work together for the benefit of the Earth and the people on Earth. We try to discover new facts about our own lives, our own bodies, in the hope that we shall be helped in communicating more easily with the Earth. We are trying to help you to perfect a machine which will be operable from our side. I think we can do it, I feel we can. There is an instrument already made, but there is some missing link, something not perfect, and we are working to see if we can make it from this side.

Myers is of course working with us for this object. There is a band formed of us who took an interest in survival and communication while we were on Earth. There are many meetings held at which we discuss both past and present developments.
You may ask, 'Where? And how do you go to them?' If I wish I can walk; on the other hand, if I have been busily engaged on other work, I can project myself in the twinkling of an eye as it is called.
I may be sitting in my own study (you mustn't worry about alterations on the Earth, I don't want my Earth study for the same purpose I did on Earth. I have one in my own house, the house I'm keeping for you).

I was changing things in his study at home.

W. F. B. As I'm sitting there I may think I ought to be at this meeting which may be a distance away in your idea; in that case I concentrate on the object of the meeting, on the place and on the idea that I ought to be there. If I concentrate strongly enough, I find myself there.
The mind can be developed on this side so that it controls the body. On your side the mind, or as much of it as functions in the physical brain, is affected by the physical body. See how the liver can affect the mind, its moods, depressing it for instance. Different states of health affect the mind to a great extent.
A severe illness or accident may put the mind out of action; but on my side the mind has power over the body – over what we call time and space; on your side the mind itself is independent of time and space, but not the brain. You can imagine yourself in America. If you've been to Shanghai you can imagine Shanghai and think yourself back there. You can't collect your physical body and deposit it immediately in Shanghai, which is precisely what we can do. I find myself at the meeting if I desire to be there, I meet my fellow workers

there and talk to them. We decide eventually on a plan of action, just as you would on Earth. Sometimes we feel there is some direction or advice that is necessary in order that we should know the best way to proceed; in that case we open our minds; in other words, we all by agreement remain silent and receptive.

Do you remember I wasn't always able to be as receptive as I should wish on Earth? I sometimes wished I could open psychically – that I could be receptive to the other world – the higher plane.

Latterly I was not always able to be passive enough in a receptive sense to take or absorb inspiration of that kind, but now I find myself able to open myself with ease to inspiration from a higher sphere than my own. The message comes – we all respond to it – we are gathered together with one mind, one idea. The fact that we have met together for a certain definite object is proof in itself that we are of one mind with regard to the object or information we are seeking, and when the call comes it does not come in the form of a voice or bell ringing. It is a mental call. One, or two, or three, or four may hear it first, before the others, according to the degree of their receptivity. We rise collectively, and those of us who have visited the higher planes before reach out to any persons who have not done so, just as you might hold out your hand in order to aid strangers along a difficult path or staircase to which they were not accustomed.

There is no feeling of danger or strangeness in it at all – none whatever; but we find ourselves ascending, the feeling is ascending. We may go to the plane immediately above our own, or even two or three planes above our own. It is undoubtedly an ascension in every sense in which we understand the word.

Myers said to me it was a reaching *out*, a travelling *out* rather than up. But I'm inclined to think that means the same thing, as the Earth is undoubtedly round, and the planes that surround it are round too; they are around it – outer rims so to speak

– so I suppose if one goes out, one goes up and vice versa; but it is undoubtedly a travelling away from one's accustomed sphere or condition.

As one travels out, one becomes aware of the different atmosphere. That I cannot quite explain to you. It is an atmosphere in which the details of one's surroundings do not seem so important as oneself, one's thoughts, and one is aware of the oneness of things – the infinite; as one travels away from the planes of finite life, finite ambitions, finite imagination, one becomes more conscious of the infinite love, infinite power and understanding, and above all, one becomes absolutely conscious that everything is working toward the ultimate good of everybody.

The further one goes out or up, the more conscious one is of this, because one draws near or nearer to the infinite source of all good. We reach what might be called another shore – yes, I will call it that – it always appears to me as being another shore. As we reach it we are conscious of the approach of other beings who hasten to welcome us. They know we have heard their call. A curious feeling comes to us as they approach us, a feeling of added power, sharpened intelligence, greater hope, greater courage comes to us like the first touch of an exhilarating wind that blows suddenly from a new quarter. Whoever these people may be does not matter at the moment, but they are those who have passed through one sphere and then another during many centuries of time as you know it. They are the teachers, the philosophers, the saints of the past. Their names are not bandied about as the names of famous people on Earth; one simply feels, 'This is a great man, he brings with him power, a great knowledge,' and yet one is dimly aware of the personal side – the glamour around them by reason of their Earth fame, and one says to oneself, 'This is So-and-so, I've read about him, I never thought I should meet him here.' But the personal side quickly takes its place in the background beside the ever-increasing interest one feels in the presence of this great soul as he is now.

INTRODUCTORY NOTE

Sometimes they take us by the hand and show us the wonderful conditions in which they live. It is an education just as travel is to people on Earth. We are shown the harmony and the beauty of this higher plane, something we are not ready for yet, but which gives us greater promise of joy to come, which we can take back with us to our own plane, and which spurs us on to further preparations for ourselves and for you. More than ever do we try to help you to live as you should live, only to do those things you should do, and to refrain from doing those things you should not do as far as possible.

The lesson of expediency is the most difficult to learn, as to how far one can carry the law of expediency and be spiritually justified in doing so. As we often tell you, motive is not everything. Principle is more important than motive. A madman may have a strong motive, a good motive for committing a crime of violence, but we must look for the principle behind the motive. That is the first lesson we learn when we arrive on this side. A man may commence from a good motive founded on a bad principle. Most wars are – each country justifies itself by its motive, but the principle of each is wrong – we have destruction. War is of no benefit or blessing to anyone. There is one work that we are incessantly striving for, and that is peace. Peace on Earth. Good will to men would create a veritable arcady on Earth – good will and peace, that's all.

It should not be difficult, and I think very often you feel my spirit helping you whenever possible on those lines. I believe you feel it.

On these higher spheres, competition, envy, personal ambition do not exist. I sometimes meet Ada on journeys to the higher spheres. She has progressed very much. Her love and sympathy for all – willing creatures to grow wings more quickly than the majority of people on her own plane.

Physical relationship isn't so important on our side as yours. There are many people in your family you will never meet again – not spiritually related at all.

Many people I knew as a boy I've never seen again, and I'm not conscious of any loss whatever – they were mere accidents of the flesh. They germinated on the same seed bed as I did, but that was all.

Afterwards they were transplanted into a place and condition of their own with which I have no connection, and that is why I have not seen and probably never will see them again. *But I want to see you* – you belong to me, we belong to each other. And Ada says, 'I do want to see you.' We must try to keep you on Earth as long as possible. You're wanted to spread the truth to help people to realise there is another life, in your own way, your own words. I do not wish you to embark on a round of spiritualistic propaganda, but here and there you can help people to understand there is another life; but the important part is not the communicating between the two spheres, but the preparing oneself for that other life, the recognition of it, that is what I want to help people to do through you.

Communication is a matter of secondary importance. It is not even advisable for everybody at their present stage of development. There are some to whom it might be a source of danger, like a drug in the hands of an ignorant and stupid person. We must recognise this, and teach the importance of preparing oneself for the spiritual life rather than the gratification of communication with the inhabitants of those higher planes. Help and guidance is always forthcoming under the right conditions.

I do want to communicate with you because I know you would only make good use of that communication. There are some people with whom I would not wish to communicate if I could.

CHAPTER 18

February 21, 1933
Leonard Sitting

W. F. B. Ada thinks also that it might be a good thing to go away somewhere this year – but remember, this appears to be a year of changes – personal changes. Don't make them, they will come to you; but don't be afraid to take them when they come.

It proved to be a year of many changes.

F. E. B. What about my scripts of messages from you?
W. F. B. You can't do anything yet, but later I shall help you to put them together and do something with them – not yet. You understand, don't you, that it is not wise to do anything yourself at present. Doing my work, editing it, is different: the result of your own personal investigations is a different matter – not wise at present.
Now, my dear, I want to say something quite seriously. I shall always be able to help you as long as you are here on the Earth. I can help you, and I can talk to you in this way. There is much we must do together, waiting for us to do together.

I have warned you of the gravity of world affairs. As you see, my warnings were justified. There is a long spell of trouble and difficulty in front of us, but we are behind you. Those with whom we are in touch, and they voluntarily with us, will be protected as far as is right and possible, unless there is some special lesson you must learn, and that you can learn in no other way than by going through a period of difficulty yourself.
F. E. B. Shall I go through one?
W. F. B. No, I don't see the necessity, but there may be people in touch with you who may still go through a difficult period as part of their education.

In giving the following message W. F. B. appeared to control the medium, speaking slowly in a deep voice.

W. F. B. (very slowly and emphatically). Let P.W. find her own way. Let her do what she wants to do, and be sure it is what she wants to do. We don't want to do anything to help her to do anything she does not want to do, only that which she feels is best for her.

Unknown to me a friend of mine, P.W., had prayed the day before that a message might be sent to her through W. F. B. to let her know if it was right for her to do the thing she wished to do. She asked me if I would read to her the notes of my sitting, but it was only after reading this script to her that she told me of her prayer.

W. F. B. We hope now she will be more free: she may have a time of greater comfort and less worry, but she must choose whatever it is she thinks best for herself.
Umbrella – I saw it the other day. You were near it, mine. You were standing near it in the corner of the hall.
F. E. B. Is it there still?
W. F. B. Yes, it should be. It *was* there. I used it a long time ago. One point is wrong in the umbrella: it's all right but for

> that, and the gumming stuff is unstuck from the inside.
> F. E. B. I'll try to find it.
> W. F. B. It has been in the hall corner behind a door. A little test – something you do not know and would not remember.

I had no idea an umbrella of his existed, but I looked for it on my return and found it where he said, and one point had come unsewn and the material stuck on the inside top had come away in places.

> W. F. B. Birthday. Two birthdays quite near. We're having a sitting near. I thought I would tell you I'm not forgetting.

His birthday and mine were in February.

June 22, 1933
Leonard Sitting

> W. F. B. I wanted to tell you today that there is still a difficult period through which you on Earth must pass; you're not through it yet. I'm not speaking personally only, but of that portion of the civilised world, and particularly this country, which is affected by the economic crisis which is not yet over. You know I've been warning you ever since I passed over about this difficult period. I did, and do know something about it. We have a most difficult time still before us, but not the most difficult as far as you are concerned and as far as some individuals are concerned, but collectively there is still much to face. One thing is that there is a spiritual hope shining through the material gloom, and we feel that it will have been well worthwhile having passed through the material crisis in order to reach the better understanding and knowledge of the things that matter. We shall gain, not lose, in the end. Those of us on my side who have definite connections with Earth, e.g. as I have with you, are helping: we are throwing in our weight, so to speak, on the right side; it will all help,

but the more or greater numbers on your side who reach out to us, the greater help we can give.

You on Earth must make the bridges: it must begin from your side – from within and below to without and upwards – that is growth and development.

You must reach out to us, the initiative must come from you: then we are allowed to give you all the help and inspiration that is possible.

I wish you were here with me, you would be interested in all that is going on.

* * * * * *

I wanted to tell you that the conclusions at which I have arrived and which I am putting in a crude and simple form so that I may put them through are these: Whatever will ultimately feed the etheric body is best assimilated by the physical in a form that can pass through the physical in as straightforward a manner as possible without involving too many metabolic changes. For instance, minerals, instead of absorbing them in a crude form as many people do, they should be taken in the vegetable kingdom and thus more easily assimilated and distributed.

It reaches and harmonises with the etheric, which raw material cannot do – this is very important.

Water, air and minerals through the vegetable kingdom are the necessaries for the upkeep of perfect balance of the physical and the etheric. Other things are valuable, but these are necessary.

F. E. B. Have you anything to tell me about healing?

W.F.B. Yes. I'm thinking of healing all the time, but what I'm telling you now should serve as a basis in a physical sense for the operation of the healing powers.

You can, I know, produce remarkable results with that healing power on poor soil without any aid through medicine or diet, but I contend you would have a greater percentage of successes

INTRODUCTORY NOTE

if you prepared the soil and made it ready for healing. There are two or three *systems of healing*. I will divide them into three.

(1) The magnetic or physical form of healing. I call it physical though the force that changes the patient is invisible, but as it is magnetic it belongs to the realm of what we call physical matter.
(2) The mental – the mind healing – the effect of one mind on another: one mind helping another to set its own natural process of healing, or even resistance, in operation.

That can be done from our side by spirit healers working through a suitable instrument on your side. That is the best and most efficacious form of mental and magnetic healing. *But* – mental healing can be done sometimes without any interference or help from our side – simply by the effect of one mind on another on the same plane. But the power is very much strengthened when it is directed by someone on my side through someone on yours.

(3) There is the third type of healing which I would call purely spiritual – a Divine healing – spiritual intercession through prayer – aspiration – or what we call consciousness of the One Mind working for the good of all.

The third type of healing may not be accessible or, I should say, may not be easily used by the average person on Earth – the two other types are used more commonly.
F. E. B. How can one use the highest?
W. F. B. I think you can use it best by realising in a definite way the power – the *complete omnipotence and omniscience of the Creat*or, and the fact – the *undoubted, undeniable fact* that whatever power He has is available to you in such measure as you can receive and use it.
The greater your capacity, the greater the work you can do. Realisation of the Divine will and love is necessary – sensing

perfection clearly, definitely – always seeing the vision of perfection.

But I maintain that while you are on the Earth you are intended to use all the assistance from the spiritual, the mental and the physical, because the physical does exist – the physical is the soil, the channel or vehicle of expression, and must be considered.

It is all very well, and sounds well to talk about spiritual being paramount, but the physical exists and is being used by the spirit and must be used on its own lines according to its necessity. I know that miracles happen in the most unlikely quarters under the most astonishing conditions, but we don't want the occasional miracle but a system of successful healing – not an isolated case here and there, but the perfect results of a perfect system – a combination of those powers which God gave us to use. But we must prepare the soil as far as possible. *Shock* [in clear direct voice.] We have to help to piece together the constructive faculties in what I must call the psychic system, so that the nervous system can operate perfectly, and set in motion the curative streams that are often available but cannot be used, as the nerves must take up the message of strength and telegraph and distribute it to whatever part of the body needs it.

I must explain something. The spiritual healing is always available; the operator may be available, but the patient may not be able to assimilate and use the healing power, which then stays in the aura instead of entering the physical organism and doing the work in a physical sense.

It is according to a patient's capacity for absorbing the healing power that the success of the healing depends, but even if the patient is in such a condition that he or she cannot make use of the power in the desired way, and it has to remain, as I said, in the aura, it will, can I say, trickle into the patient's body in some measure – it will help, but the operator or director of the power cannot ensure a complete and entire assimilation on the part of the patient.

INTRODUCTORY NOTE

Another important point: you may meet with cases in which a patient passes over while being treated in this manner. Do not think such a case is a complete failure. If you could only follow the passage of that patient's etheric body to our side you would see with the greatest satisfaction the tremendous help given in freeing the etheric body from the impression of illness.

Where there has been shock we find it difficult to be sure of the readjustment of the physical and etheric bodies. In the physical the nervous system is something to be reckoned with, a very troublesome factor, yet capable of being a very helpful one if it can be adjusted and made to respond to the promptings of spirit and mind.

The brain being the medium through which consciousness – i.e. *spirit* and mind combined – works, anything that has caused a shock to the nervous system, the handmaiden of the brain, makes our work very difficult. That is why we always impress you to avoid shock of any kind.

The strange thing is that a gradual series of events taken in their cumulative effect may only result in beneficial action on the same person to whom a lesser number of those events concentrated in too short a space of time will constitute an injury or shock.

A shock is only a certain number of causes concentrated in too short a space of time which should have been spread over a longer period.

Take a change caused by a surgical operation. In a short space of time certain changes have been effected in a phenomenal way one must call it – this causes a definite shock to the system.

The same effect may be produced by what we call natural causes over a long period; the same result and change might be produced without the shock.

Where there has been a sudden shock we find it difficult to apply the spiritual healing power – we can apply it, but it is more difficult.

December 1, 1933
Leonard Sitting

W. F. B. Do you realise I have been able to help you, giving you mental support when you needed it? That is the one legitimate way in which we can help you.
We give you confidence – you must always choose the way yourself. It is very difficult, but it is your task to choose. It is the choosing, the finding the right way that strengthens your character and soul forces and fits you for life.
Be prepared for readjustments, but they will be all right. Don't jump at them – only take them when you reach them, or they reach you. Changes and readjustments are things for you to take quietly, and only when you must. When they are indicated take them fearlessly, but don't create too many if you can help it.
There is a woman on the Earth whom Ada's helping too – a difficult case. This will be all right. We must not try to act the part of Providence. We must act and think as seems most helpful from day to day.
She's been ill some time. You know we should like her on this side, in one sense we should rejoice if she came today. I should thank God, it would be easier for her. But though I would thank God if she came today, I don't want to choose God's way for Him.
So many of us are working round you now to help – people whom you knew on Earth, but with whom you never expected to work – they gather round you forming a kind of spiritual bodyguard, so to speak. You would be surprised if you saw and recognised some of them.
Don't let anyone worry you about publishing work or writing of mine or about me. When it can be, and you feel like it, I shall be glad, and shall help.
But don't let anyone rush things. I think people need it now – the message. We shall do the work. There are two distinct sets of work:

INTRODUCTORY NOTE

(*1*) Connected almost entirely with material I collected – there is plenty of it.
(*2*) The material you have collected from me.

F. E. B. Which do you think is more important?
W. F. B. The second – it's the newer and the more alive.
You see there are several of us trying to get this material through – there must be many who have tried, and a few who have succeeded in giving information of the same type, but what has been done with it? Has it come through to your side or has it failed to do so? And again, if it has been recorded, is it wasted by being ignored – not understood? Some recorders may have passed over before they could publish it, and in that case it is all wasted.
I feel the world needs a signpost at the cross roads which evolution has now reached.
Evolution has indeed reached the cross roads, and there is a right route and a wrong route, and we must play our part in writing clear directions – pointing in the right direction.
Humanity is not travelling in an ordinary quiet way towards these cross roads: it's dashing – hurtling towards them, and there will be many crashes, but – but, my dear, there will be many also who will pull up when they see the signpost, and it will save them; and as they turn in the direction to which the signpost points others will follow them.
The signpost must indicate that there is a definite route to immortality.
F. E. B. Where does the other route lead?
W. F. B. I was going to say destruction, but I will not say that: delay, chaos, disharmony, unhappiness – a dark road the further you go along it.
Now then, if we can play our part in erecting the signpost we shall have done the best we can for our fellow creatures. Never before in history has humanity needed a sign as it does now. I want to help you to do this.

You know it's not just the evidential side of communication that counts – people have had a great deal of that; they want to know this: if we live, how we live. And what do we consider the best way they can live in order to make the best of life before passing and after – the two sides of the picture.

This has been in your mind too, your mind has been awakening to the possibility of undertaking this task, though I think you must co-operate with it.

It is a case of a lot of work to be done in editing these messages – posthumous communication. (I dislike being identified with posthumous.) I'm living, I'm more alive than I have ever been. I'm happy because I have entered the fuller life without being ashamed to do so, and I'm able to enjoy it, and I'm in touch with you – that completes my sense of happiness. You are not too unhappy. Your talks with me, and even more, your realisation of my nearness, my love and my understanding have helped you. They have given you a new light on life.

Ada says the difference in you from twenty years ago is that previously you were actuated by a sense of duty – now you are actuated by a sense of the divine, which is a greater and more blessed thing and I hope that in publishing this work, you will assist people to take the first rung of the spiritual ladder.

F. E. B. What is the first rung?

W. F. B. The first rung is looking above self. I ought not to suggest *forgetting* oneself; getting above oneself means realising one's higher self, and reviewing and controlling one's lower self. But one is on the top of it, and the higher on the ladder one climbs the more easily is one on the top of it. Even if we fall down again, and we often do, we can climb more easily for having tried and failed.

In more senses than one we know the ropes: those who will not try never know what they can do. Go ahead without fear: what you do for the best as far as you can see it will lead you in the right direction – will be best for you as well as for other people.

INTRODUCTORY NOTE

Don't let too many people draw on you and monopolise you in a wasteful way.

If there is any definite way in which you can advise and help, do it, but so many people fritter away time and energy, and that is more tiring to you than work. Lately I've seen you more tired after an hour with people in meaningless chatter than after an hour's strenuous work: it's depressing too.

There is satisfaction in an hour's work, but you take nothing from an hour's chatter.

When this work is done there will still be more work for you to do. You're not going yet, but it's not in my hands. I'm told always to help you to get certain things done on Earth, therefore I judge you are not coming for some time.

George is here. You know he is helping his wife – doing all he can.

F. E. B. Have you any message from him?

W.F.B. You will not understand it yourself. Quite recently she has been thinking of a place where they were long ago, and they were very happy; it was their early days together – Chester – Chester is part of the name.

They lived in Edinburgh from 1908 to 1910, and it was there the decision was made to accept the post in Manchester.

They were not there very long, but she thought of it recently and he was with her and he remembered how happy they were, and at the same time they were making a very important change – taking a serious step while they were in contact with that place. The place is not so important in itself; it was the things that happened about that time that were important, and she was thinking of it and so was George recently.

He – George – has met a man also connected with the same conditions. [He has passed over.] Ask her if she remembers the name Nicholson.

This man has a connection with that place and period. [I give this only as evidence.]

Professor Nicholson, George's economic chief in Edinburgh, had recently died.

CHAPTER 19

February 22, 1934
Leonard Sitting

W. F. B. Is there a little difficulty in the mind of a friend of yours? She would love to speak to Ada, but in her mind is a feeling – not against the subject, but just a little fear it may not always be right to do it. She's got that feeling.
I would like you to tell her from me she is right: it isn't always right for people on your side to communicate with ours: people on your side are not always spiritually ready: many may be psychic, but if not spiritually ready to use the power they often hurt themselves and others by trying to step in where angels fear to tread.
There are many highly developed spirits here who are most careful in the way they try to communicate with Earth, and people on your side should be equally careful of their motives and their spiritual attitude toward the whole subject.
Vic [direct voice]. Someone is saying this.
F. E. B. Who?
W. F. B. Not an old man. *Vic* [direct voice]. He is middle aged I should say.
F. E. B. How did this man pass over?

W. F. B. Suddenly. Something with his head. He was unconscious when he passed – not lately – some years ago.

This was quite unexpected by me. It correctly describes a man very devoted to Vic (a friend of mine), who in a fit of African fever took his own life.

W. F. B. *Will.*

Direct voice.

F. E. B. Did you say Will?
W. F. B. *Yes, not your Will.* He wants to speak to her. He has been trying to get in touch with her. He came to you through another medium, but you didn't recognise him, but mixed up the name with me.

That is true. Someone gave the name 'Will' at another sitting, but obviously it was not W.F.B.

W. F. B. I think I'm remarkably fortunate in being able to see and hear through you, as I do. So many on my side are limited to doing and seeing so little of the Earth side of life, and after all, the Earth life is valuable experience – vitally necessary to our development, or God would not have made the Earth and placed us on it. He meant it for a testing place for our soul's development, and the reason we are told to pray against violent death is that it deprives us of the opportunity to get our souls full experience.
We should not die young, but should live as long as we can to get full experience and development on the Earth in a spiritual, mental and material way.
If not so, what would be the value of health, or trying to attain health, also medicine or laws of hygiene? We might drift along in any way. This is an important subject, and you are the very one through whom I can work and impress people

INTRODUCTORY NOTE

of the importance of perfecting the physical life, existence, and possibilities of expressing it in happiness and education – I mean spiritual education.

Some time ago I told you I was trying to understand the cause and the remedy for cancer. I am going ahead, but I am attacking the cause.

I'm not looking for a germ, but I am looking for the breeding ground that allows such conditions – destructive conditions – to manifest.

I think we shall find we have got to confine ourselves to the one issue – clean blood – and I want to get if I can a few simple instructions which I hope to impress on you – a few simple rules which we can hand on to prevent the growth of this terrible scourge.

When I have extended my studies a little further I shall be able to tell you the result, but I'm afraid it will be so simple, so straightforward, that no one will want to follow it.

So far as I can see at the moment the whole solution rests on keeping and maintaining internal cleanliness, not by artificial means, but naturally. It is very important.

F. E. B. What do you mean by natural means?

W. F. B. Through the channel God meant to feed the body. To create clean blood through the food we eat and the liquid we drink. I should say not one person in ten is absorbing the food that would maintain the blood in pure condition.

F. E. B. What food?

W. F. B. That is what I am trying to find out – to make a table I can give you. I may have it next time you come. A few things to take and a few things to avoid.

I think the explanation will be extremely simple, and the treatment.

I'm amazed at the number of cases where people have died of diseases originating in toxic poisoning generated in impure intestinal conditions. There is the root of all evils flesh is heir to. You know we are magnifying the importance of brain, heart, lungs, kidneys, liver – the three first we have taken to be the seat of so much trouble and disease. They are not: they are the regions where symptoms manifest themselves according to individual tendencies. They are not producing areas, but the regions in which symptoms are likely to manifest and cause trouble.

From birth – in earliest infancy, the intestines are the important part of the anatomy. They are the seat of disease. They are the area from which good or bad health springs in every case like the one we were speaking of today. We can trace it to bad conditions of the intestines years ago, sometimes in childhood.

I'm trying to find out the pure foods nature demands in order that we should keep our physical organisms in good working condition.

You see the difficulty we shall have in this: we cannot go back to the nut eating, the wild herb eating, which I suspect nature knew was right for us. In the centuries we've changed part of the mechanism of our bodies, so they couldn't now deal with those raw materials, and it may be never again shall we be able to digest such things, and probably we shall be a finer race – a more perfectly formed race – through having developed our tastes along lines only remotely connected with the abilities of our forefathers in dealing with the nuts and weeds and grass and coarse kind of vegetation that came from the land and the bed of the ocean.

I understand we have lost a great deal of valuable food material that at one time man took from the bed of the ocean, whether in deep or shallow water I am not sure; but in historical records the vegetable food that man got from the sea has been confused with fish. We – as we progressed – concentrated on catching and eating fish, and we've ignored the most valuable product of the sea – vegetation. We are discovering it to a certain extent now.

I'm waiting for you and preparing a place and I think you'll like it – garden – and I'll tell you the name, long and unpronounceable, of every bush and plant and everything that grows in it.

I wish you were here.

INTRODUCTORY NOTE

November 2, 1934
Leonard Sitting

Speaking of the messages given through Mrs. Leonard and of their possible publication, W. F. B. said:

W. F. B. There is so much material, but I only want you to use that which will carry conviction to the intelligent and unbiassed reader. There is some extraneous material we shall have to cut out. I wish to use any evidential material, but I would like to link up the actual evidence with material that might not be called evidential in itself, but which we should have every excuse for using, e.g. sidelights on the beyond, especially anything that provides evidence of personality and the persistence of individual tastes and the possible gratification of those tastes.
I would like to speak of music, of art in its various forms, of the colour and beauty of form in our world; facilities for friendly co-operation, a better social system, and last – but not least to me – the opportunity for botanical research, trees and plants; all that life so beautiful here, it interested me, as you know.
I should like you to insert side by side with the purely evidential and veridical matter anything that shows the persistence of surroundings, and opportunity for the indulgence of individual tastes and pursuits. Music—.
F. E. B. But I don't think you have ever spoken of music in these sittings.
W. F. B. I want to speak of it today, that is why I have introduced the subject.
The music you know on Earth is nothing compared to that we know here. We have not only the examples of music of the last few centuries, but we have the music that has been lost to us in civilised times, I say civilised, but it is a wrong word, a misnomer, because music and art of thousands of years ago were wonderful and they have been lost – only a dim memory inspires us.

Here we have the music of *ancient* Egypt: it is lost to you on Earth.

Just imagine – I have met so many of the composers and heard them conduct their own works; I mean the composers of our times.

A curious thing – it seems that while one is on Earth one's brain, which is inhabited by that part of the mind we call conscious, is always on guard against anything it regards as being outside its own range.

Anyhow – outside its own range appears to be what we have learnt to call supernormal or supernatural, and the lower, more conscious mind instinctively rejects it, works against it. This is the habit formed by centuries of tendency to think on certain lines.

July 16, 1935
Leonard Sitting

W. F. B. Edith speaking – she wanted to send a message to her son.

E. Give S. my love: tell him I am watching over him. He was thinking of me so much yesterday. He was thinking of when he was younger and of the letters – his letters. Something reminded him of them – his letters to me, he has been thinking of them lately.

And a *little*, very little photograph of me, he didn't know it existed. He seemed surprised – a small one. I do not know if he or someone else found it, but he looked at it surprised, as if he said, 'I didn't know it was hers.'

Tell him I am just the same as I used to be. He was wondering how I looked, what land of body, whether I was tangible – had a tangible body.

Tell him, 'Yes, I have, and when he comes to this side, whenever that time comes, he will be able to see and touch and hear me.'

I knew nothing of the meaning of these messages till later when I saw S. He then told me he had been turning out E.'s bureau and had found letters which he had written to her from France during the war. They were carefully tied together. Also his sister had found a photograph of her taken in her garden and had sent it to him. In it she was a tiny figure, but it was vividly like her. Neither he nor I had known that such a photograph existed.

> E. Darling, did you feel me on Sunday? I tried to impress you that I was with you. In the morning the singing of the birds. I heard the birds, one especially well, he sang a solo outside.
> I loved Sunday morning. I went somewhere with you later. Didn't you remember? It made you think of my passing. Sunday – music! I wish you could hear mine.

On the Sunday before I was at Lady Margaret Hall, Oxford, and lay in bed early in the morning listening to the birds, and one bird seemed to be singing all the solos and the rest the choruses.

Later I was at a very wonderful International Service in Christ Church. The time was the anniversary of E.'s passing in 1934.

> W. F. B. I must speak for a moment on world conditions, because in a sense they will affect you. There is a temporary lull in war conditions, but it is not ended; there is bound to be trouble, not only with Italy but with Germany.
> F. E. B. Do you mean war?
> W. F. B. I do not think England will be seriously involved, or not so much as other countries, but a very difficult position is facing England and I do not know quite what will happen, or how she will come out of it.
> F. E. B. What ought England to do?
> W. F. B. Keep out of things, but though I say she should do so in the future, she should not make rash promises that afterwards she must break – faith that she cannot keep: that has happened in this late war. She has been compelled to fail

another nation, and allow the enemy of that nation to prevail in spite of given word – a bond that was made.

It will be a lesson not to enter into pacts and promises she is not able to fulfil. Her inability and that of other countries to fulfil their obligations will place them in a different position for the future. You will see I am right.

There is now no real co-operation or unity. The policy in Germany is very bad. Do you know we are helping, doing what we can with those driven out and persecuted? We have been helping them, and taking charge of those who have passed over.

W. F. B. I've been very much with you on a new plane and footing. I think you recognise that. I have been connected with the guiding, strengthening, helping and guarding you on the lines upon which you have been desiring guidance.

You are travelling by the road I indicated some time ago. I told you that you would do less of your own professional work on orthodox lines, and it is coming to pass that you are doing so, and it is right.

Don't be afraid, give yourself up; you will get not only guidance in that way, but also peace: we shall be nearer and closer in thought. Go on – just be ready. Don't seek to know the plan too far ahead, because it must be changed from time to time. Do as I told you before: ask for *this* day's guidance. You have been doing that. I am working with you in it, and Ada and Edith.

* * * * * *

You have still some work to do here helping in the more spiritual sense.

The world has drawn away from God; help is needed to teach people to give themselves back to God.

Win all the people you can, bring them in, we are with you, it's our work: the work of proving survival is important; but we cannot let things rest there, it must mean something

INTRODUCTORY NOTE

to us, and to you: it is really working in God's service that you are doing now and have to do. It is giving yourself up to God and obeying Him. Do it thoroughly and help people to discard all those things that are not of God.

I am helping you, it is our work too. We do it on this side; it may interest you to know it is part of our daily programme. Don't feel you are failing in other directions.

Rid yourself of any unnecessary responsibilities. God does not wish you to be burdened. He wishes you to be free for His service.

Do you notice the material things are falling into line so as to fit in with this comparatively new work? It is good for the body and good for the mind. On the Earth that which is good for the mind is practically certain to be good for the spirit. It is a spiritual movement in the world which is bringing God into things, and it also brings things and people to God. The world and God are being drawn closer together.

Spirit and Creative mind are one and the same thing with God. Spirit and Creative mind are God and God seeks to express himself through us. We have to give ourselves to Him in order that He may express himself through us. Then we become of *God*, we become one with God, and we are safe and all whom we bring to Him on those lines are safe.

F. E. B. What do you mean by safe?

W. F. B. At rest, at peace.

'Thou wilt keep him in perfect peace whose mind is stayed on Thee'; when your mind is stayed on Him, it means you've given yourself to Him. That is what I mean by safety; you live and function in perfect peace. I can wait in peace for you now I am working with you in these things: I am side by side with you.

Doesn't the world need God? You remember I told you there would be great changes. I have been warning you for years that terrible things would happen. They are happening, and all are needed. Each one drawn in will be another soul safe – I want to use that word – in God's harbour. His service is

His harbour. Not safe in the selfish and personal sense, but in the broader, larger sense.

Go on with your friends: encourage and help. I am in full sympathy.

You might think fun is dead on our side. We have more fun than ever we did on Earth, but kind, good fun, laughing with people instead of laughing at them.

* * * * * *

Do you remember what I predicted some years ago? I said to you that the Kingdom of God would come on Earth, that the hidden truth of the Scriptures so essentially simple would be lived today, revealed in all its simple and wonderful beauty as a great oneness – unity – through a daily and hourly endeavour of each to unite oneself with God, the great purpose behind and in everything.

It is so simple, we are clarifying it now, revealing God simply as He is.

Go on, without fear, steadily, happily, filling in the time till you join us.

Epilogue

To many readers of these scripts proof of survival of personality is the primary problem, to some the only interest, yet for others it would, if proven, have a secondary value too, for without it there is no standard by which to judge of such glimpses as can be given us of life in another sphere. Such glimpses must depend for their content on the communicator's personal experience of it, and will vary accordingly.

Some critics have suggested that varying descriptions of another world which have been given by different communicators prove that none of them are veridical, but even in our own world the African Chief who came to England in a big liner and stayed at Buckingham Palace with the 'Great White King' found it quite impossible by picturesque language or other method to convey to his people any conception of what he had seen and experienced, so different was life in Central Africa from life in a great city like London, though in the same world.

The value of what is given to us in messages will be influenced, therefore, by whether the sender has been able to convince us of the survival of his personality, and will then be only an approximation to his own knowledge and experience.

It will have been noticed by the reader, too, that in the sitting of Feb. 8, 1927, W. F. B. further explains that only a part of the consciousness is able to get through into Earth conditions.

In Myers' *Human Personality*, page 334, he asks,

What then is to be our conception of identity prolonged beyond the tomb? In Earth life the actual body, in itself but a subordinate element in our thought of our friend, did yet by its physical continuity override as a symbol of identity all lapses of memory, all changes of the character within.
'Yet it was memory and character – the stored impressions upon which he reacted, and his specific mode of reaction which made our veritable friend. How much of memory, how much of character, must he preserve for our recognition? Do we ask that he or we should remember always, or should remember all? Do we ask that his memory should be expanded into omniscience and his character elevated into divinity? And whatever heights he may attain, do we demand that he should reveal them to us? Are the limitations of our material world no barrier to him?

Memory and character – it is possible to discuss whether these few extracts from communications over a long period give any evidence of their persistence, but first there is a more intangible kind of evidence which should be mentioned, though only those who have had personal experience of similar sittings can appreciate it. In a Leonard Sitting we cannot see the visible form and the changing expressions that used to come and go with interest in discussion; we cannot hear the spoken voice with the exception of the few whispered words and sentences in direct voice; we cannot feel the grasp of the well-known hand; but though sight, hearing and touch are excluded, we can and do get a sense of the presence of our friend in a way that must be experienced in order to be realised.

This sounds the most elusive and deceptive of all modes of recognition, yet I have known men of sceptical mind, previously sure that telepathy from the mind of the sitter explains all, become absolutely convinced of their friend's presence in a sitting, though everything said was already known to the sitter; yet veridical messages given through a proxy sitter who had no knowledge of their truth or value has carried no conviction to the same person. Such conviction, however, cannot be passed on to others; it concerns the individual alone who has had the special experience.

But, as Myers suggested, there are elements in what we describe as personality which can be estimated apart altogether from physical or psychical manifestation – the elements of character and memory. Broadly speaking, character includes the interests of the individual concerned, the knowledge and skill possessed by him, his methods of conveying ideas to others, his reaction to things transcendental, e.g. religion. Still more convincing to some perhaps would be the persistence of memory – memory of events, particularly of events in which he alone was concerned.

It is because the messages here briefly recorded suggest the survival of the personality of W. F. B. from these points of view that it has been thought worthwhile to publish them.

Consider in his case the interests, knowledge, skill, reaction to transcendental thought and philosophy which revealed his character.

His primary interest in life was the science of physics. Secondary interests were psychical research and horticulture, and in later years medical science from an outside point of view.

Research in any subject meant for him exactness in method combined with an open mind, ready to accept only what is absolutely proven, irrespective of preconceived ideas.

I think it would be admitted that he had skill in the use of words – clarity without redundancy; and in parts of the script where the communicator seemed to have obtained almost complete control of the medium, this characteristic will be recognised.

In teaching or explaining a subject to those with less knowledge of it than himself he was wont to convey somewhat abstruse ideas by the use of simple concrete illustrations.

This method is to be found in parts of the script, the examples being drawn chiefly from physics or botany, both subjects of primary interest to him.

Coupled with this is the recognition of the similarity of law throughout nature.

Another feature is the interest from the first in things of the spirit and an ever-increasing anxiety for the recognition in the world of today of the importance of the spiritual life in man.

There is manifest in many places that humility of soul which was so characteristic of him; e.g. 'Myers and I are learning many things together, and I from him.'

'We believe – with Myers it's knowledge.'

Again the recognition of the 'privilege' to meet and see those in more advanced spheres.

But the most convincing details of memory and ways of speaking are too personal for publication.

On one occasion he spoke in the sitting of an intimate friend and told him the names by which I used to address him, explaining that though it was embarrassing to him to speak of private things he did it as being evidential, since it was unknown to the sitter.

The names were correct though unusual.

The answer given to my first question in the sitting of September 1925 as to how he could prove that it was W. F. B. himself communicating is very typical of his thought, viz. that it depended on the calibre of the mind who was to be convinced – different minds requiring different types of proof – broad lines of interest in the case of Sir Oliver Lodge, trivial facts which were identifiable in the case of others, selfish interests in the case of enquirers of lesser calibre.

Many will recognise the avoidance, where it could be achieved, of the possibility of explanation by telepathy, and the use of any opportunity given by sitting with another medium to show that the intelligence directing discussion of a subject is not to be found in the personality of the medium.

The ready response by some critics to this suggestion would be, 'No, it would be more likely to originate in the mind of the sitter.' But that explanation is excluded when a message is sent through a medium who does not understand its meaning, no sitters being present. (November 5, 1929, Bazett.) Also when the sitter was my secretary with no knowledge of the incidents he claimed to have observed, he recognised the value of this fact from an evidential point of view.

EPILOGUE

But there is a wider proof of character which can only be appreciated by those who knew W. F. B. He was never bound and fettered by preconceived ideas, but pursued the wider issue.

When psychical research claimed his interest – even subjects which at first seemed to him too trivial and absurd to waste time on, as when asked by the Society to investigate Dowsing, he agreed to give his leisure time for a few months, but in that short time he found that new facts came into view that demanded an open mind, further study and observation.

A scientific colleague once met him after a lecture he had given on telepathy and greeted him with 'A very interesting lecture, Barrett, but it's all tosh you know.' He replied, 'Well, you are a scientific man; when you have given as many weeks as I have given years to the investigation of these subjects I shall value your opinion.' The quick and generous reply was, 'You're quite right, I have no right to an opinion, but I will give some time to it myself.' The result was a similar conviction of the value of such research.

Spiritualism never claimed him as a Spiritualist – for him psychical study included not primarily the question of survival, but wider aspects of the psychology of man. In a day when science was largely against the truth of Christian religion he retained his belief and experience of the reality of the spiritual life in the larger sense, which he maintained was not antagonistic to knowledge, but was that whole of which scientific knowledge is a part.

In these messages from time to time attempts are made to prove his survival and knowledge of Earth life by many trivial incidents, but he still lays chief emphasis on the contention that even scientific proof of survival is not the most necessary end to be attained. Far more important is it for man to realise that the object of life on Earth is the development and evolution of human qualities and the birth of the spiritual life in the human without which the life that is to come will be a much harder experience.

One realises, however, that to many the consideration of messages which purport to come from some intangible world which interpenetrates our own seems the greatest folly. To such I can only quote Blanco White's sonnet on 'Night and Death.'

Mysterious Night! when our first parent knew
Thee by report Divine and heard thy name,
Did he not tremble for this goodly frame,
This glorious canopy of light and blue?
But through a curtain of translucent dew
Hesperus with the host of heaven came
Bathed in the hues of the great setting flame,
And lo! Creation broadened to man's view.
Who could have guessed such darkness lay concealed
Within thy beams, O Sun, or who divined,
When flower, and leaf, and insect lay revealed,
That to such countless worlds hadst made us blind?
Why should we then shun death with anxious strife?
If Light could thus deceive, wherefore not Life?

Blanco White.